WHAT I WORE TODAY

Graffito Books
32 Great Sutton Street
Clerkenwell
London
EC1V 0NB
UK

www.graffitobooks.com

Design: Astrid Kogler
Production: Yak El-Droubie

Printed in Portugal

ISBN: 978-0-9553398-7-5
British Library cataloguing-in-publication data
A catalogue record of this book is available at the British Library

WHAT I WORE TODAY

FASHION REMIXED ONLINE
FROM BEIJING TO BERLIN

GRAFFITO

WWW.GRAFFITOBOOKS.COM

★ **above left** johanna > Vallentuna > Sweden
★ **above right** madison > OH > USA
★ **below left** vlada > St Paul, MN > USA
★ **below right** michelle > Wayville > Australia
★ **facing page** hannah > Wilmington, NC > USA

CONTENTS

★ above katie > Southampton > UK
★ above right julia > Des Plaines, IL > USA
★ facing page cris > Chicago, IL > USA
★ below right angela luisa > Los Alamitos, CA > USA
★ below left rebecca > Cincinnati, OH > USA

INTRODUCTION

Real fashion photos posted online are transforming the way we dress. Women from L.A. to London, Tokyo to Senegal are standing in front of the camera and taking control of their image. The diversity of real life fresh fashion posted online on a daily basis offers endless inspiration. Difference and individuality are celebrated, permission to experiment granted. Outfits are chosen, mixed and remixed, to reflect the day's mood. This is about living creatively. For 10 minutes, when the camera is positioned, the outfit adjusted, the backdrop and props chosen, the room cleared of roommates, boyfriends and pets (or not, as is sometimes the case), the pose struck, the women in these photos capture themselves, or an aspect of themselves – who they are that day. They then present it, unmediated by anyone else, to the world, by posting it online.

Couture is mixed with thrift, mainstream mixed with hand made, vintage mixed with something borrowed from a sister's wardrobe. Online, the diffusion and sharing of style is instant – someone in Bangkok can see and be influenced by what someone in Chicago put on that morning and vice-versa. Street-fast-fashion is no longer dictated by access to cool neighbourhoods, catwalk shows and underground parties but can be open to all those who have an internet connection and know where to look – so someone in Slovakia can be as stylish as someone in New York City and someone in Beijing can pollinate the style of someone in Paris, who then pollinates the style of someone in Helsinki – and the fashion world gets smaller and more globally infectious.

Fashion rules are unpicked, broken and rebuilt and photos are accompanied by a burst of contrasting viewpoints and opinions. Alongside the juxtaposition of trends, tribes and fashions, these photos give a glimpse into hundreds of different worlds. Refreshingly self-assured, open and creative, the individuals included here are all different, all inspiring, thanks to them for sharing what they wore.

This is probably my most favorite thrift store find! I found it last weekend at Goodwill when my friend Jason came to visit. I wasn't in the shopping mood, but Jason convinced me to go, and then of course within minutes I stumbled upon this dress!

E...

anana Republic
an Outfitters
falling apart green mary janes
o

"Going to buy Easter eggs!
Or maybe a bunny, I haven't
decided yet."

WHAT I WORE...

★ black opaque stockings from the
  supermarket. they're nearing the end
  of their life, i'm afraid!
★ yellow OTK socks sock-dreams.com
★ black leather and suede 1970s boots
  with buckle detail
★ white lace/cotton dress Target. also
  nearing the end of its life :(
★ my very favorite blazer thrifted for
  eight dollars last year. made by 'Table
  Eight'. i replaced the original buttons
  with brass military buttons.
★ crown brooch 99 cents on Ebay!
★ 1960s aurora borealis brooch part of
  my grandmother's costume jewelry
  collection that i inherited
★ vintage silk Kenzo scarf in
  'Harlequin' print

WHAT I WORE…

★ peach pure wool cardigan vintage,
  Etsy.com
★ bow blouse thrifted, Fida
  charity shop
★ blue belt thrifted, UFF
★ skirt Camilla Norrback
  (i sewed it to fit higher on the waist)
★ shoes Vagabond
★ eyeglasses YSL

WHAT I WORE...

this is my impersonation of rich bitch
face. apologies.
vintage 70s silk dress from my
mother has two labels: 'Ola
Designs' & Henri Bendel
Martinez Valero kitten heel
my mother's belt
cardigan from who knows ?

WHAT I WORE...

- ★ **bow** American Apparel scarf
- ★ **shirt** Goodwill by the lb
- ★ **blazer** Steve and Barry's
- ★ **black deim skinnies** F21
- ★ **boots** Aerosoles, christmas gift from mom

WHAT I WORE...

red bow handmade
white blouse Forever 21
baby doll jumper H&M
red bow belt Wet Seal
navy tights Walmart
red patent slingbacks Hot Topic
red bag Urban Outfitters

WHAT I WORE...

★ scarf thrifted
★ shirt Target
★ skirt thrifted
★ tights Walmart
★ heels DSW
★ earrings Walmart

WHAT I WORE...

TOP: this is the cheesy farm girl pin-up outfit. it earned me my first and only wolf whistle when i wore it last year.
★ shirt H&M
★ shorts thrifted. sadly a bit too small to be comfortable. i'm on the hunt for more similar shorts that fit me better.
★ belt my boyfriend
★ shoes hand me down from my aunt. one of my favorite pairs.

MIDDLE:
★ top Ebay
★ skirt Ebay
★ belt flea market
★ tights Lindex probably

"Today is my birthday!"

BOTTOM:
★ dress Ebay
★ stockings What Katie Did
★ belt flea market find
★ shoes a gift
★ purse Ebay
★ a bunch of pearl necklaces

"I'm visiting family today. This is one of my favorite nooks of my grandmother's attic! Today I'm channeling the 1930s... Yesterday we went to see Atonement, and I just can't get it out of my head!"

WHAT I WORE...

★ scarf Oona's
★ dress The Dressing Room
★ bag Salvation Army
★ tights Macy's
★ vintage Palizzio shoes – one of the many beau
   pairs i inherited from a close family friend

16

"I found this cute jumper last week. The colors are so illustrative that I paired it up with a striped silk blouse."

WHAT I WORE...

★ b+w silk top thrifted
★ 80s/early 90s jumper thrifted
★ purple wooden necklace thrifted
★ rose cuff thrifted
★ black ankle boots thrifted

WHAT I WORE...

★ shirt, jeans, shoes Target
★ sweater Ebay
★ scarf gift – my sister brought me this cashmere Buffalo checked scarf back from New York, it's my new favorite!

WHAT I WORE...

plaid Timberland men's shirt charity shop

brown shorts Topshop (ages ago) and my
mother made them short

black woolly tights unknown

blue knee socks Primark

gray fuzzy Ugg style boots Primark

red pashmina some stall in London maybe

gold disc earrings a boutique in Paris

various bangles and bracelets unknown

dad's watch

green parka jacket (on chair) Primark

"A tidy room! Spending a sunny
day with my parents.

"Dorothy's shoes?"

WHAT I WORE...

★ **shirt** a gift, tag says 'Betty Boop'
★ **skirt** vintage, used to be my grandmother's
★ **shoes** Deva

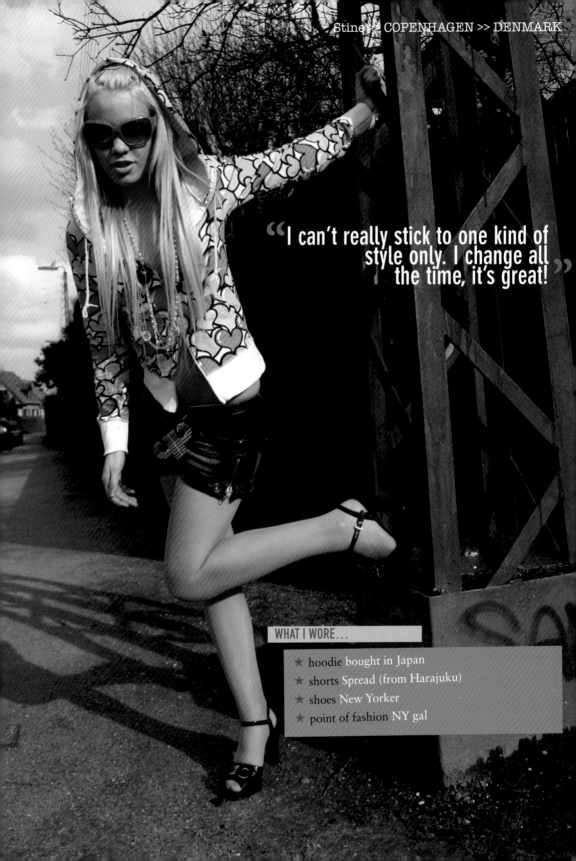

"I can't really stick to one kind of style only. I change all the time, it's great!"

WHAT I WORE...

★ hoodie bought in Japan
★ shorts Spread (from Harajuku)
★ shoes New Yorker
★ point of fashion NY gal

WHAT I WORE...

★ Dame Edna-esque glasses China
★ tee H&M
★ skirt online
★ black crinoline petticoat China
★ belt Zara
★ bag H&M
★ shoes H&M

WHAT I WORE...

★ **dress** small shop in Copenhagen
★ **belt** stitches
★ **leggings** American Eagle
★ **beads** Urban Planet

summertime!
↪ dress **Mango,** but i changed the straps
from the middle to the edges
↪ necklace **Animal**
↪ shoes **Gola**

24

WHAT I WORE...

★ vintage top some store for $8
★ chocolate leggings Target
★ gold sandals thrifted and remixed a million times
★ peach paint mixed by me

"Clouds and drizzle"

WHAT I WORE…

…to school on a gray sky morning
★ shirt, jeans, shoes Target
★ pink (and very cute) voodoo necklace
Takashimaya
★ white lace camisole Samuel & Kelvin
★ pale camouflage shorts Fox
★ gray leggings online spree
★ brown cloth flats Mondo
★ brown (and very faded) bag Bugis Village

AT I WORE…

✶ the skirt i wore yesterday too. it's actually just below knee length, and comes up to the waist. yesterday i rolled the waist band to make it shorter. last night i tacked parts of the hem to the inside of the waist band for a different look. it's easy to do, and i can simply take the stitches out and wear it long again if i want.

tank Urban Outfitters
tights Vera Wang for Kohl's
thigh highs American Apparel
shoes (moccasins, falling apart) thrifted

Lydia >> ABBY, BC, CANADA

TOP: this is one of my favorite pieces of clothes...that sometimes forget about. i thrifted it in the 10th grade think), back when my best friend Katie and i would g to Value Village and get the ugliest things we could fi and see if we could get away with it. everyone told m was a Bill Cosby sweater, but i loved it regardless. eve time i've worn it in the past six months, i've gotten cc pliments, which shows the effect of fashion and trend

- ★ cardi Value Village, $5
- ★ tee Joe remixed
- ★ jeans remixed Target
- ★ shoes Gap, $12 (you can't see the green gingham but they're adorable :D)
- ★ bow scarf, $4, Target

MIDDLE: four eyes, again. soooo i managed to lc my last pair of contacts and had to wear my glass boo hiss. luckily, the lady at my optometrist is goi to give me a pair until my pack comes in...thanks Joyce!

- ★ tee remixed, Work
- ★ vest Value Village, $4
- ★ skirt remixed, thrifted
- ★ scarf thrifted, 25 cents
- ★ shoes Value Village, $6

BOTTOM: i think my outfit today is comple thrifted!

- ★ dress actually a skirt which is basically the white version of my trusty black skirt, Salvation Army, $4
- ★ slip remixed, Value Village
- ★ cardi Value Village, $8
- ★ belt scarf, $3, Value Village

WHAT I WORE...

★ bronze sandals Target
★ skirt Salvation Army
★ cardigan my favorite Lutheran thrift
   store

"The strawberries are breakfast"

WHAT I WORE...

★ **dress** vintage. did i mention i love pleats?

★ **belt** thrifted

★ **boots** thrifted

★ **scarf** Claire's i think

WHAT I WORE...

★ cardigan secondhand
★ shirt The Beautiful Ones
★ skirt American Apparel
★ shoes vintage
★ sunglasses vintage

…AT I WORE…

…OP: ★ hair in a POMP! (ozone? what ozone?!)
★ leather rose necklace
★ black dress Portmans (new)
★ turquoise cardigan Topshop, buttoned behind
   my back as a faux-bolero
★ black stockings
★ black boots (new) the rose print on them
   matches my necklace! eye for detail, me (wink)
★ lucite bracelets & TT ring

…IDDLE: ★ purple silk scarf fashioned into turban
★ big bug sunglasses
★ green vintage dress bought in San Francisco for
   next-to-nothing
★ purple lamé leggings American Apparel
★ black wedges Alexandre Herchcovitch for Melissa
★ Tarina Tarantino rings

…OTTOM: today i am channelling Diana Vreeland/
…tle Edie — hence the serious face!
…ll, Diana/Edie if they were alive today… a
…uristic reincarnation, maybe.

★ pink scarf
★ house of flying daggers dress World
★ cardigan Ricochet (only buttoned at the
   top)
★ Manolo Blahnik black heels (swoon)
★ three clear lucite bangles, new obsession
★ Tarina Tarantino skull ring

WHAT I WORE...

★ skirt, jacket, shoes thrifted
★ tee, socks gifts from my husband

WHAT I WORE...

★ cardigan Express
★ white shirt Forever 21
★ burnt sienna skirt gifted
★ teal boots gifted

WHAT I WORE...

finally, a better picture of the lovely nautical
dress i got. this one does the dress far better
justice

★ dress vintage via Ebay
★ skirt (navy, under) American Eagle
   customized by me
★ shoes secondhand
★ bag gift
★ belt vintage

"I Love This Dress,
Yes I Do

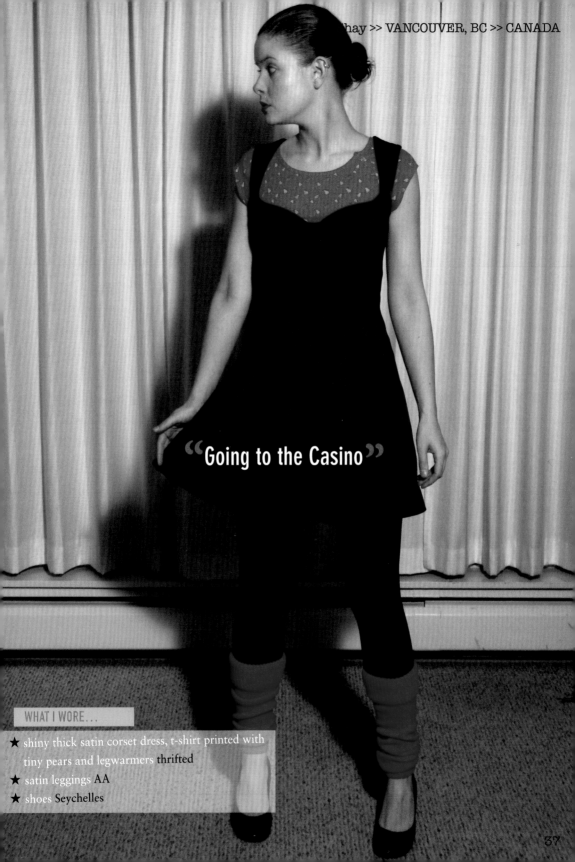

"Going to the Casino"

WHAT I WORE...

★ shiny thick satin corset dress, t-shirt printed with
   tiny pears and legwarmers thrifted
★ satin leggings AA
★ shoes Seychelles

"i try my best to be super cute XDDD"

WHAT I WORE...

ABOVE: happy times
★ t-shirt handmade
★ cardigan second-   hand
★ tights H&M kids
★ scarf gift
★ shoes DNW

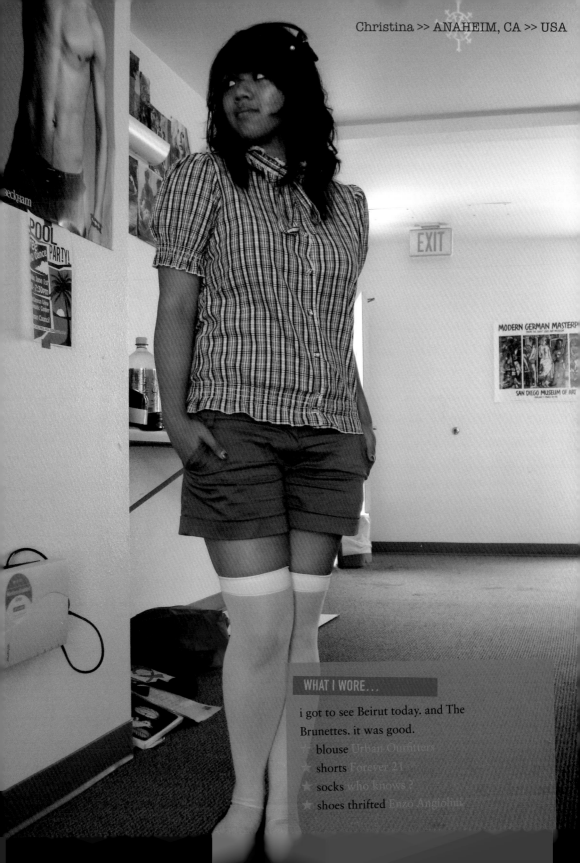

EXIT

MODERN GERMAN MASTERP

SAN DIEGO MUSEUM OF ART

POOL
PARTY!

WHAT I WORE...

i got to see Beirut today. and The
Brunettes. it was good.

★ blouse Urban Outfitters
★ shorts Forever 21
★ socks who knows ?
★ shoes thrifted Enzo Angiolini

WHAT I WORE...

★ cardigan H&M
★ tank Bikbok
★ skirt/suspenders F21
★ tights New Oldstock
★ shoes Bronx
★ button Starstyling, Berlin

WHAT I WORE...

★ dress vintage 1960s
★ necklace vintage (hard to see amidst the crazy print)
★ bracelets vintage
★ bag Chloé
★ sandals Prada

"Off to check out the antique wares on Antique Row"

"Red medicine"

WHAT I WORE...

today, floral dress. what i´m laughing
at? such a mystery...
★ dress thrifted
★ cardigan very old Zara
★ tights department store
★ ankle boots a downtown shoe
  shop, i can´t remember the name
★ purse thrifted

WHAT I WORE...

★ ivory crepe chiffon blouse Seductions
★ black lace camisole Eaton's i've had it since highschool
★ beige plaid wool pleated skirt thrifted
★ frye 'lisa' oxfords UO online
★ 1950s Pancho 'Gorgo' Gonzales tennis racquet thrifted

"Kate Hepburn wouldn't even give you a chance"

taking a short break from posting bread pictures...this pose proved to be surprisingly comfortable. as for the picture, my face is quite strange, but the body pose warranted posting.

WHAT I WORE...

★ **scarf, vest, belt** thrifted from Salvation
  Army, remixed

★ **tee shirt** hubby's old, it shrank

★ **necklace** thrifted from Saks

★ **cut offs** made from old thrifted jeans,
  remixed

★ **leggings** old, not sure, remixed

★ **loafers** thrifted from Goodwill

"Travelling day...for real this time."

WHAT I WORE...

★ cognac shrunken leather pea-coat
Banana Republic
★ gray stripes sheer knit hoodie
TJMaxx
★ turquoise cami don't know
★ straight leg stretch denim Earl Jean
★ ugly boot Simple, remixed
★ feeling:
cute: 4
functional: 5
creative: 2

Edward Hopper

WHAT I WORE...

i'm forever blowing bubbles
- ★ dress made out of a thrifted nightgown
- ★ socks local store
- ★ shoes free section at the local flea market

WHAT I WORE...

blue and white striped dress vintage
scarf Chinatown
belt Forever 21-type store
purse Target
shoes Macy's

I really like this photo because of the mural
but also because my boyfriend took this
for me right after we picked up tacos for
dinner!

" Inspiration: I'm reading Brideshead Revisited and this outfit is inspired by the cover of the library copy I'm reading and also the whole idea of rich dandy college boy drunks in the 20s.

WHAT I WORE...

★ shirt kid's uniform shirt, Goodwill
★ skirt and needlepoint bag my favorite
   thrift store in town
★ tights thrifted, new
★ "R" pin garage sale
★ shoes Thrift and Dollar in Aurora IL
★ watch antique store
★ bakelite ring Ebay

"The bathtub and the stripey dress"

WHAT I WORE...

TOP: after a huge night...
- ★ hooded shirt **Cotton On**
- ★ dress **Sportsgirl**
- ★ tights **thrifted**
- ★ socks **don't know**
- ★ shoes **BigW**
- ★ inspiration **a little bit hip hop, a little bit High School Musical and a little bit Hairspray. I've got a little bit of a crush on Zac Efron right now (sooo dirty).**

MIDDLE: ★ navy singlet **Sportsgirl (my sister's)**
- ★ blue floral wallpaper skirt **altered and thrifted (it was heinous old lady shorts – elasticized and everything)**
- ★ mustard tights **Grab?**
- ★ yellow-orange flower **thrifted**
- ★ white peep-toes **thrifted**
- ★ navy handbag **thrifted**
- ★ silver chain **Target ($3)**
- ★ pearl necklace **can't remember**
- ★ ridiculous sad/serious face **i just looked at the carpet.**

BOTTOM: ★ necklaces **vintage**
- ★ corsage **St Vinnies, Gladstone Road**
- ★ corset-shirt **vintage, it was a dress but it was too Morticia Adams**
- ★ net-belt **vintage, i have no idea what it actually is, i think its meant to be a headband**
- ★ high-waisted shorts **vintage**
- ★ tights **Target**
- ★ shoes **some random shoe store**
- ★ inspiration **cruises, SJP and the lovely Beth from The Vintage Society**

WHAT I WORE...

everything is from Salvation Army

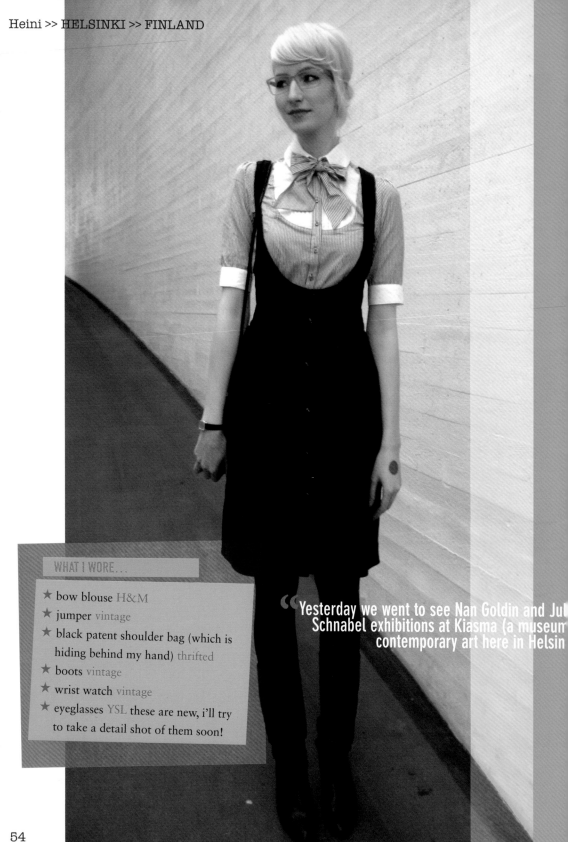

WHAT I WORE...

★ bow blouse H&M
★ jumper vintage
★ black patent shoulder bag (which is hiding behind my hand) thrifted
★ boots vintage
★ wrist watch vintage
★ eyeglasses YSL these are new, i'll try to take a detail shot of them soon!

"Yesterday we went to see Nan Goldin and Ju Schnabel exhibitions at Kiasma (a museum contemporary art here in Helsin

WHAT I WORE...

TOP: ★ vintage floral dress thrifted years ago
★ headband don't know
★ brooch with Mary Pickford photo thrifted!
★ super-thick opaques to keep from being immodest can't remember
★ vintage black/white/red brogues Ebay
★ bag Ebay

MIDDLE: ★ cashmere beret Target sale
★ jumper thrifted
★ underskirt – eons-old Delia's
★ overskirt – vintage 1940s skating skirt (for real!) Ebay
★ thigh-highs Sock Dreams
★ leather/suede burgundy stacked wood heel oxfords – vintage 70s, Ebay (seriously most comfy shoes ever)
★ Edwardian locket

BOTTOM: this is probably my most treasured dress ever. i missed my bus taking these shots!
★ vintage 1930s crepe 'sea anemone' dress Ebay
★ belt thrifted
★ scarf thrifted
★ wool cardi Ebay
★ tights Target
★ brogues Ebay
★ rucksack Ebay

Natalie >> DOWNER >> AUSTRALIA

"This dress was made for someone a lot taller than me, and so I have to take it up soon."

WHAT I WORE...

★ 1950s pink and gray silk striped dress with black velvet trim
★ pink cardigan, i.e. the cheapest cardigan in the world not sure where i got it
★ black kitten heels Novo
★ black bow tie pilfered from my mother recently

JE

JE T'AIME

WHAT I WORE...

★ dress H&M (bio cotton)
★ shoes Keds
★ bag (Louison inspired)
★ the cat-model Malo, my lovely cat

"Pouty panda.
Dressed up for my friend
"zoo party

WHAT I WORE...

★ panda hat Little Raccoon via
  Fred Flare
★ b+w mod dress Urban Outfitters
★ black tights Conway
★ black oxfords Target

WHAT I WORE...

★ suspender skirt Insight
★ tunic LA Made
★ leggings AA
★ red headband F21
★ nameplate necklace Helpless Romantic
★ boots Fluevog
★ thrifted German mug

"Here is my new 80s dress. I had no idea how perfect it was till I got home. It even has a bubble skirt that poofs on it's own.

WHAT I WORE...

★ dress thrift
★ shoes Walmart

WHAT I WORE...

TOP: excuse the messy room!
★ gray and white gingham dress Target
★ brown belt Target
★ brown moccasins Steve Madden
★ brown expandable clutch thrift

MIDDLE: very warm in Virginia today.
warm enough to make me lazy enough to
not care about flat ironing my hair.
★ gray headband some sort of cheap
   drugstore brand
★ gray tank Old Navy
★ rust tunic Patrick Robinson for Target
★ silver locket H&M
★ jeans H&M
★ unseen silver/leather flip flops
   Charlotte Russe

BOTTOM: just wore this dress a little over a
week ago, (see above) but it's so hot in Virginia
that it was the only thing really bearable to
wear! i'm guessing it's definitely going to be
THE summer dress for me. also, it shrunk a
little in the wash, and got even cuter! plus, it's
definitely wrinkled, but i think it looks cute that
way.
★ gray gingham dress Target
★ brown belt thrift
★ brown bag Bitten by SJP
★ navy open-toed flats Target

WHAT I WORE...

★ vintage ship 'n shore tee my mom's
★ vintage denim skirt thrifted
★ vintage sandals thrifted
★ giant red bag yard sale $1
★ bird necklace flea market

WHAT I WORE...

★ tunic Gap
★ pants thrifted
★ fake Keds Target (during the day at the
   office i wore leopard flats but these i
   wore going to and fro, and this pic was
   taken right when i got home)

WHAT I WORE...

★ glasses H&M
★ blouse Sh Atmosphere
★ cardi Click Fashion
★ skirt Sh
★ tights H&M
★ peep-toes Deichmann
★ bag Reserved
★ belt Sh

WHAT I WORE...

this is my new photo spot, since i'm now self employed and working at home, yay! it's going to take a bit more effort to get some nice outfits on instead of the PJs!

★ cardigan my own design for the company i used to work for
★ bead necklace vintage
★ dress old dress from sale rack at Urban Outfitters
★ slip vintage
★ socks gift from my friend from Tokyo
★ shoes vintage

"This was my holiday Monday garb

WHAT I WORE...

★ zebra shirt Urban Outfitters
★ tank Old Navy
★ gray jeans Old Navy
★ boots Blowfish

"Green Machine"

WHAT I WORE...

★ cardi one of my FAV's from
   Hong Kong
★ orange tank thrifted
★ white pull-over 5-7-9
★ skinny jeans no name gift
   from sister
★ sandals thrifted

WHAT I WORE...

★ shirt Comme ca ism (Tokyo)
★ mini small shop in Hong Kong
★ outer Uniqlo (Tokyo)
★ heels small shop in Hong Kong
★ rosette necklace Paris Kids (Tokyo)
★ two-tone belt Gracious Ground
   (Tokyo)

WHAT I WORE...

i get sooo excited whenever Target
starts a new GO International line!
two white v-necks Forever 21
gray/metallic high waisted skirt
Target GO International
leggings thrifted
purple heels thrifted
sunglasses UO

"Boyz in the Hood
in the background.
Word."

WHAT I WORE...

★ **dress** made by my sister
★ **purse** thrifted
★ **scarf** thrifted
★ **shoes** thrifted

Johanna >> TURKU >> FINLAND

WHAT I WORE...

★ black earrings Glitter
★ black plastic pearls Only
★ black + white striped t-shirt H&M
★ red purse H&M
★ black bracelets H&M
★ violet skirt H&M
★ black tricot skirt H&M
★ red tights Lindex
★ black shoes DinSko (second hand)

WHAT I WORE...

TOP: yellow!! it was so nice out today that no
other color but yellow would do!
★ yellow cami Old Navy
★ black cami Charlotte Russe
★ skirt Wet Seal
★ shoes Payless

BOTTOM:
★ shirt Pac Sun
★ dress Delia's
★ tights Charlotte Russe
★ shoes DSW

**"Happy Valentines Day! Now I have a good excuse to
wear pink and red together! And some black, 'cause
love sucks sometimes. And it was waaay to cold to
just wear the dress by itself!"**

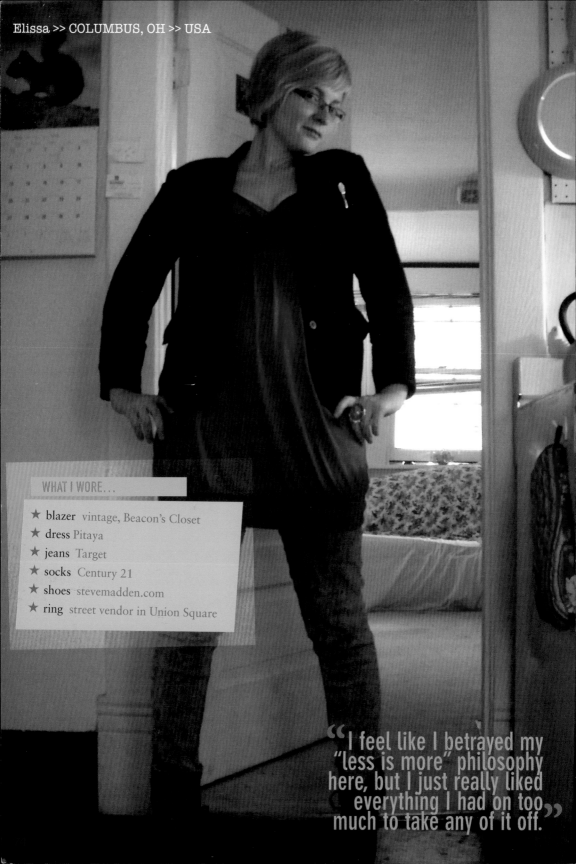

WHAT I WORE...

★ blazer vintage, Beacon's Closet
★ dress Pitaya
★ jeans Target
★ socks Century 21
★ shoes stevemadden.com
★ ring street vendor in Union Square

"I feel like I betrayed my "less is more" philosophy here, but I just really liked everything I had on too much to take any of it off."

"I know I wear this skirt too much, but it's yellow and I have a really bad thing with yellow skirts, (I love them too much). But this top I hardly ever wear, actually I've only worn it out once before so I thought I'd bring it back from the dead. The shoes are my boyfriend's I just slipped them on for this shot."

"Pink Hallway"

TOP: 60s red and white. i wore this when i was
babysitting
★ hairband was originally used on a present someone
  in my family got
★ earrings bought in Paris
★ shirt my mother grew out of it and gave it to me
★ belt i think it used to be my sister's
★ skirt vintage
★ tights anywhere...
★ shoes Din Sko

TOP MIDDLE: gloomy. i was home being sad and
lonely today when my best girlfriend called and
asked if i wanted to meet up later so i put on some
nicer clothes for the occasion
★ flower (in hair) from mum
★ scarf had it forever
★ dress American Apparel
★ skirt boyfriend's mother's old
★ tights anywhere

BOTTOM MIDDLE: the sixties returns (even though
my hair is too short to do a proper beehive with now).
the dress has a lovely backside so i had to take a
picture of it
★ dress Beyond Retro (vintage)
★ tights Indiska
★ shoes Din Sko

BOTTOM: when i was little i always wanted to be
an air hostess because of their pretty uniforms
★ hairband from childhood
★ scarf mum's old
★ shirt thrifted
★ dress thrifted (from Finland!)
★ lunch box my sister's
★ tights anywhere...
★ shoes mum's old (so they're a bit big for me...i've
  got tiny feet)

WHAT I WORE...

★ all thrifted
★ except socks, those were from Target

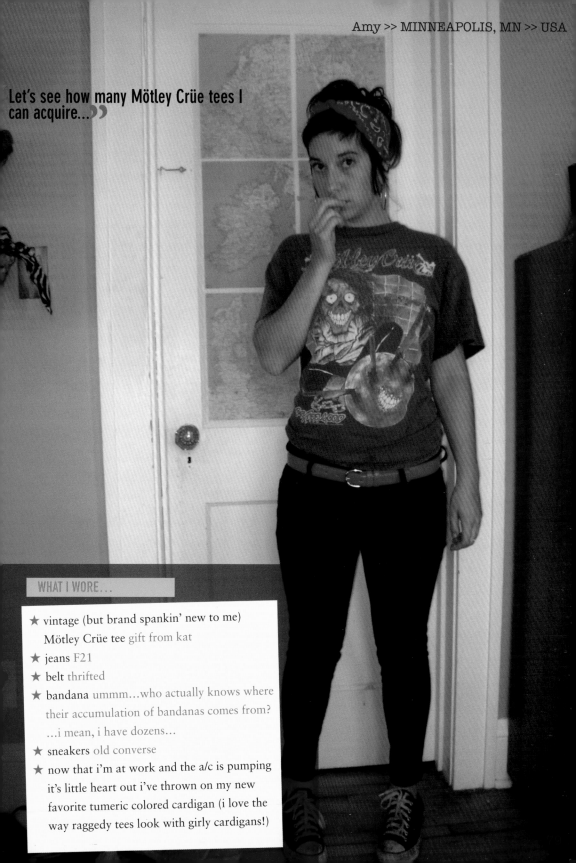

Let's see how many Mötley Crüe tees I can acquire...**"**

WHAT I WORE...

★ vintage (but brand spankin' new to me)
   Mötley Crüe tee gift from kat
★ jeans F21
★ belt thrifted
★ bandana ummm...who actually knows where
   their accumulation of bandanas comes from?
   ...i mean, i have dozens...
★ sneakers old converse
★ now that i'm at work and the a/c is pumping
   it's little heart out i've thrown on my new
   favorite tumeric colored cardigan (i love the
   way raggedy tees look with girly cardigans!)

"I flit,

I float"

WHAT I WORE...

self-timer photos from today with balloons left over
from a charity event
★ Cardigan Forever 21
★ Blouse Anthropologie
★ Jeans Abercrombie Kids

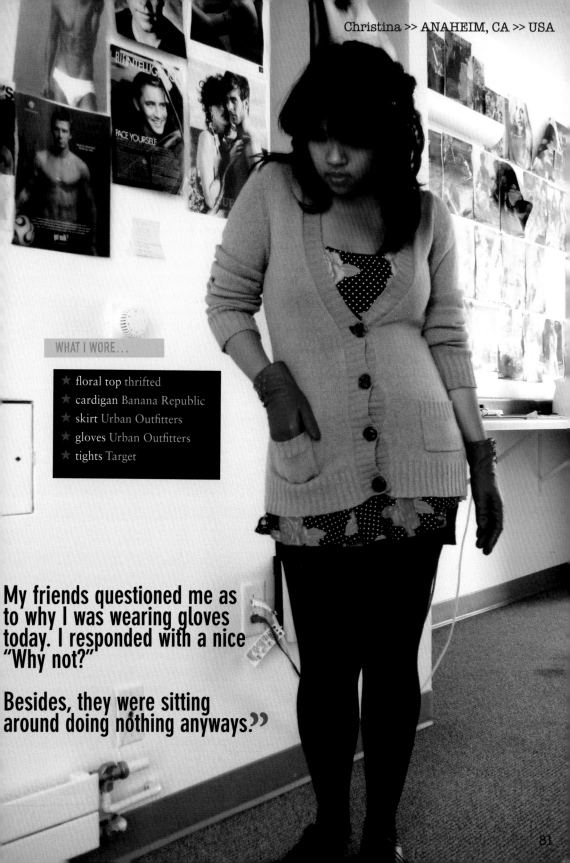

WHAT I WORE...

★ floral top thrifted
★ cardigan Banana Republic
★ skirt Urban Outfitters
★ gloves Urban Outfitters
★ tights Target

My friends questioned me as to why I was wearing gloves today. I responded with a nice "Why not?"

Besides, they were sitting around doing nothing anyways."

WHAT I WORE...

★ plaid button-down thrifted
★ grey tank thrifted
★ belt thrifted
★ black skirt cut the sleeves off of a
   long sleeve tee (i believe i got it F21?)
   to wear as a skirt
★ plaid tights can't remember

"Last day of March today. It's slightly rainy out will be tomorrow as well...but tomorrow's go be nearly 65, and even though it will be rainin know I will be beaming on the first day of Ap

WHAT I WORE...

the lumberjack skirt
★ coat Vivienne's collection
★ hoodie (underneath) Miss Shop
★ skirt Ralph Lauren
★ boots RMK

WHAT I WORE...

★ i am wearing a blue/white striped
sleeveless shirt with white collar (was
my grandfather's)

★ the scarf was my grandmother's

★ cardigan Benetton

★ jeans Sinequanone

★ shoes Pedro Garcia

"My sister was making me laugh!"

WHAT I WORE...

★ **blouse** thrifted, vintage
★ **belt** sister
★ **skirt** from mum
★ **tights** from sister
★ **shoes** $4 from Target
★ **headband** 40 cents from Target
★ **peep bow coat** DFO sale
★ **funny sister**

WHAT I WORE...

magenta!
★ jacket small shop
★ dress H&M
★ tights somewhere in Tokyo
★ booties somewhere in HK
★ bag vintage (without tag, but
  believed to be Versace??)

WHAT I WORE...

TOP: i thrifted this skirt yesterday, i safety pinned it to give it a bubble effect, i just wore it like this around the house
★ tye die skirt thrifted
★ black patent leather belt thrifted/remixed
★ black bodysuit with jewels thrifted
★ Ferragamos remixed
★ 50s cats eye blue glasses with my prescription Ebay

MIDDLE: i am trying not to get stung by a bee, tons of black bumble bees!
★ 70s wool plaid skirt thrifted
★ blue turtleneck H&M
★ boots, sunglasses, bag remixed

BOTTOM: had this skirt a while, but got confused with what top to wear with it
★ floral denim skirt thrifted
★ blue suede belt remixed
★ yellow striped top thrifted
★ heart necklace thrifted
★ fishnets thrifted
★ Feragamos remixed
★ sunglasses remixed

"I just had to show you the back of the dress since it's the best part!"

WHAT I WORE...

★ butterfly necklace Joy in
   Clapham Junction
★ ring engagement ring from c. 1910
★ red dress from a boutique on
   Upper Street
★ leggings Uniqlo
★ red shoes vintage from Spitlefields
   Market
★ glasses Red or Dead

"Doll dress"

WHAT I WORE…

★ dress H&M
★ pullover Monoprix
★ shoes Chie Mihara

this is what i will wear tomorrow for
church (i know i wouldn't have time to
take it tomorrow!)

★ San Francisco tee and velvet high-waist
  skirt hand me down from mom

"Today dress code for architecture student supposed to be khaki pants and white shirt, but I decided to add some pink, umm... many pink ;)

WHAT I WORE...

TOP: ★ t-shirt pink babydoll Zara
★ white shirt Contempo
★ cardigan Jennifer Adler
★ pants Mango
★ belt Alun Alun Indonesia
★ shoes my dirty tracce shoes

MIDDLE: i'm going to Laos (café) to meet my girlfriends. Since we're just gonna talk all night, i decided to wear something cozy and slouchy...
★ t-shirt bag and stripe shirt thrifted
★ stripe babydoll Shot
★ shoes Charles & Keith
★ tights Depato in Jakarta

BOTTOM: its Monday morning. i'm excited to go to campus today, i have a morning class (7.30am)
★ mom's basic shirt
★ secondhand balloon skirt
★ knit bolero from factory outlet
★ Zara shoes and Roxy bag from high school era...

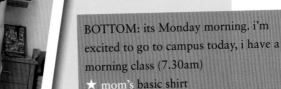

WHAT I WORE...

★ i found this dress underneath a huge
pile of clothes in my closet, it's a
bit wrinkly but it suited me fine for
a trip to the farmer's market for
grocery shopping

"Mi primer intento como striper"

¿enseñar el conejo contará como foto de striper de las que pedía Jose?

¿ir en camisón a currar me acerca más a mi ideal de convertirme en Diablo Coldy o me encamina directa a la cola del paro?

mientras resuelvo mis dudas, otra foto

WHAT I WORE...

Dara's senior show was today and i was her date, so i had to get fancy and funky. all the college students seemed to like it, so i deem this outfit a success!

★ shirt thrifted
★ belt thrifted
★ skirt thrifted
★ tights drug store
★ shoe Target

"Dara's Senior Show"

WHAT I WORE...

still in the tacky mood. i look really
something (ethnicity wise) in this picture,
but i can't pick out what it is. i really love
the color rose near my face since it tends
to bring out the pinks in my face (lips,
cheeks, and eyes)
★ cropped hoody JC Penny
★ shirts Ross
★ shorts Walmart
★ socks and head band Wet Seal
★ flats Nu Pair

"walking the cat!
lol my face"

WHAT I WORE...

★ lace dress Salvation Army
★ belt My Friend's Closet thrift shop
★ sweater American Apparel
★ boots Salvation Army

"You're a painting with symbols deep."

WHAT I WORE...

★ pistachio shirt Miss Selfridge
★ embellished top Dunnes
★ skirt/dress passed on from a friend
★ purple tights can't remember
★ plum wedges Aldo
★ hair pin steenink.etsy.com

WHAT I WORE...

this jacket is so awesome, i just adore it! i love European clothes. it's wool, a bit like felt, so it's nice and warm. the edges are all raw and the design is so unusual. i just know i'll wear it all the time.

★ earrings Diva
★ Line 7 shirt Beechworth Emporium
★ Italian wool jacket Mon Amore Paris, Toorak Village
★ 18th Amendment Colbert jeans shopbop.com
★ red patent leather platform heels Marina Mirage
★ red bag Alannah Hill

WHAT I WORE...

i'm really excited to be wearing my new
heels with my old dress
★ dress vintage
★ belt vintage
★ shoes Madden Girl

"It's finally started raining again in Vancouver! Looks like it's going to be a whole week of rain. I love it."

WHAT I WORE...

lazer pug and Family Guy
★ konichiwa t-shirt Urban Outfitters
★ deep U dress AA
★ nylons Winners
★ brown boots vintage from Ebay
   (LOVE THEM!!!)
★ silver sparkle belt Claire's
★ lazer pug free with photo!

WHAT I WORE...

★ hat, jacket, blouse, pants and boots
all thrifted
★ tank and socks Target

Stephanie >> SINGAPORE

WHAT I WORE...

- ★ tee Topman
- ★ necklace paraphernalia.nu
- ★ belt Zara
- ★ skirt online
- ★ black crinoline petticoat China
- ★ socks H&M
- ★ shoes Philippines
- ★ bag H&M

WHAT I WORE...

TOP: ruin of old school
★ skirt dress, bag H&M
★ jacket Fishbone
★ boots Rylko

BOTTOM: secret garden
★ bonnet mum's wardrobe
★ skirt A0misu
★ jacket H&M
★ shoes Zara
★ earrings selfmade

"I've dreamt about this dress. In Poland wasn't my size. I get it from Italy."

"Nothing like starting the day off by throwing up in the office in the middle of a conversation with your boss. No, I wasn't hungover. Anyway, today was pretty great! New bicycle = my love."

WHAT I WORE...

★ cowboy boots from my mom
★ black tights
★ grey skirt from H&M
★ black pullover bought years ago
★ necklace gift from my boyfriend

WHAT I WORE...

★ **all** thrifted

"Am I bright enough??"

WHAT I WORE...

★ jacket Alfani
★ shirt Zara
★ skirt H.Naoto (i love this skirt, it has little cherubs on it)
★ petticoat Ebay
★ tights i can't remember
★ boots Frye

"Summer, y'all. Also, fever, so i am not even sure what's going on temperature wise."

WHAT I WORE...

- scarf some asian grocery store
- vest an ex leftover
- sweater H&M (dudes')
- jeans don't know
- shoes Keep

WHAT I WORE…

★ gold hoops thrifted
★ gray felt flowers hat thrifted
★ thick warm wool scarf thrifted
★ pin of cats on a fence with moon and stars thrifted
★ brown tweedish blazer old navy
★ hot pink wool skirt thrifted
★ brown cotton skirt Filene's Basement
★ black cotton skirt ragstock
★ green socks thrifted
★ black fuzzy boots urban outfitters circa 1999

WHAT I WORE...

- ★ gray beret by the lovely Tara-Lynn
  of yarnovermovement on Etsy
- ★ winged tiger head necklace
  pickypicky on Etsy
- ★ white tee American Apparel
  black jumper dress santokivintage
  on Etsy
  mustard tights American Apparel
- ★ boots vintage Ebay

WHAT I WORE...

TOP:
- ★ **dress** F21
- ★ **scarf** thrifted
- ★ **socks** Target
- ★ **flats** originally bought from Buffalo Exchange, but i bought them off my friend cause they didn't fit her.

TOP MIDDLE:
- ★ **sweater** thrifted by my best friend, handed down to me. it's sort of ill-fitting but i really don't care too much
- ★ **shorts** Hollister jeans from 10th grade cut into shorts. looking back i would have went with a darker wash jean instead but those shorts were probably in the laundry!
- ★ **shoes** gift
- ★ **sunnies** also a gift

BOTTOM MIDDLE:
- ★ **coat** an amazing find buried underneath other clothes at F21, only $40!

BOTTOM:
- ★ **shirt** Erin Fetherston for Target
- ★ **bubble skirt** thrifted
- ★ **socks** Toys R Us
- ★ **shoes** Shop More? Pay Less!

Alegra >> CHICO, CA >> USA

" Rainy day. Went thrifting for pieces to use for a cosplay. "

WHAT I WORE...
★ all pieces remixed
★ i totally forget where the skully tee came from...

WHAT I WORE...

★ high waist skirt with pockets vintage
★ t-shirt American Apparel
★ shoes vintage
★ sunglasses vintage

WHAT I WORE...

⋆ top Forever 21 (it was a dress and i
   put it in the dryer – now it's a shirt)
⋆ jeans Superfine
⋆ scarves vintage
⋆ boots vintage
⋆ bag H&M

"Old lacy mc racy.
For a long day you need something that makes you feel good. but also that you can run about town in.. i'm totally digging having brought back this shruggy-bolero-ish thing back from Glasgow."

WHAT I WORE...

★ shruggy-bolero-ish thing Next clearance (it cost 1 pound 25 yo)
★ belt my boyfriend's mum's
★ top Topshop
★ trousers Mango
★ shoes Primark, but i love them...

WHAT I WORE…

day two of curl hawk. i used a different setting lotion.

★ sea urchin earrings
★ brown vintage shirt with floofy bow
★ red shrug from Target, 2005
★ brown skirt from 1940s suit
★ red leather gloves estate sale
★ red socks Urban Outfitters San Francisco
★ brown shoes from Target, 2004

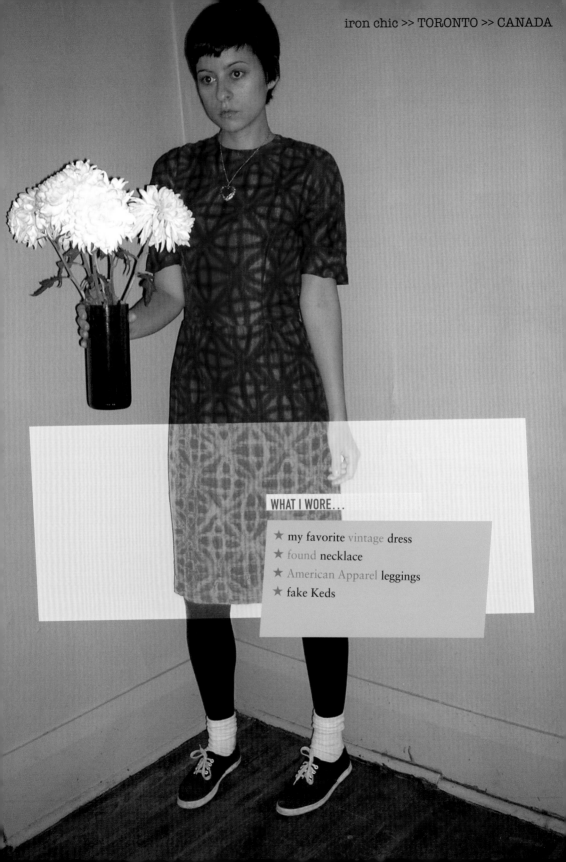

WHAT I WORE...

★ my favorite vintage dress
★ found necklace
★ American Apparel leggings
★ fake Keds

WHAT I WORE…

TOP: it was so hot this past weekend. i'm glad it cooled up enough for me to wear a jacket
★ plaid men's shirt, jean jacket, oxfords remixed
★ mustard stirrup leggings thrifted, The Value Center
★ Janet Jackson 'Rhythm Nation' t-shirt Ebay, BlackLuna Vintage
★ P.S. i'm a big Janet fan, so i was super happy when i saw Black Luna's auction for this shirt

BOTTOM: i am human and i need to be loved
★ red Smiths' 'meat is murder' t-shirt thrift store on Highland Ave
★ orange mini skirt H&M ($1!!!)
★ tan leather belt with gold buckle thrifted, Valley Thrift Store
★ tights, navy cardigan and oxfords are remixed

❝Going out two days in a row is not something I
very often. But going to two crazy LA fashion ever
in one week is something I know I'll never be ab
to do agai

My friend Nick got a bunch of us on the list for th
finale show for LA Fashion Week. And it was held
Union Station; which made it more exciting for n
because I love that place. But the clothes wei
um, interestin

WHAT I WORE...

shirt vintage
skirt vintage
shoes nine west

WHAT I WORE...

★ **shirt** Sex Pot ReVeNGe
★ **overall shorts** bought on a vacation to Spain
★ **over knees** bought in a 300 yen shop in Japan
★ **shoes** Dosch (from Harajuku)
★ **point of fashion** ghoulish with a twist of VK

"Late picture
was pretty busy today
sigh"

WHAT I WORE...

★ shirt **Black Milk**
★ skirt **Sarah Heartbo**
★ tights **unknown**
★ shoes **Pleaser**

WHAT I WORE...

★ navy and white vintage dress Ebay
   (shortened)
★ rusty tights H&M
★ shoes vintage
★ eyeglasses YSL

126

"unfortunately, the pictu
where the dog licked t
camera didn't tu
out we

WHAT I WORE...

★ shirt dad's closet
★ skirt vintage
★ socks Sockdreams
★ shoes cheapies I've worn before
★ earrings thrifted
★ dog out of frame

Erica >> MANKATO, MN >> USA

WHAT I WORE...

★ **dress** Target clearance racks
★ **cardi** thrift store
★ **leggings** Target
★ **shoes** Target
★ **dog** borrowed to increase the cuteness of the picture!

WHAT I WORE...

going out dancing!
★ the dress was actually a gift from Naja
   Conrad Hansen, a Danish illustrator
   and artist: meannorth.com

WHAT I WORE...

- ★ shirt Oasis
- ★ skirt GT
- ★ tights H&M
- ★ shoes somewhere cheap in London
- ★ scarf Pieces
- ★ hairclips Glitter

"In my parent's house's attic.
Scary old mannequin feet
standing around."

WHAT I WORE...

black and blue
★ hood Official Tourist
★ t-shirt American Apparel
★ puffy shorts H&M
★ shoes Cheapo

WHAT I WORE...

Shane got a new bike with antique brass rims yo! so classy! it inspired this crazy flapper-esque outfit

★ 80s polkadot dress thrifted
★ polkadot blouse Seductions
★ flapper headband i made it from 80s sequin belt and an ostrich feather
★ victorian cameo brooch Ebay
★ fishnet kneehighs! the bay
★ 90s Guess boots thrifted

"Bike tricks"

Johanna >> TURKU >> FINLAND

WHAT I WORE...

★ black heart-shaped earrings Glitter
★ silver necklace with character J a gift
★ corset top Vero Moda
★ black tulle skirt H&M
★ black tights H&M
★ red high-heeled shoes Seppälä
★ red bag H&M

WHAT I WORE...

TOP:
★ bunny-ears!
★ silver sequinned Disney ears
★ silver earrings Sportsgirl
★ American Apparel sweater
★ skirt Ricochet (NZ)
★ silver mesh heels Nine West
★ blue gem Tarina Tarantino ring
★ 'GALA' initial rings Girlprops

MIDDLE:
★ bunny-ears!
★ Hello Kitty hairclip
★ blue silk dress a weird hippie shop
★ pink silk dress Topshop (this has full-
    length sleeves which i rolled to different
    heights)
★ falling apart wedges
★ Hello Kitty wristband Kaia
★ toy handcuffs bought in London
★ = outfit to meet friend in the botanical
    gardens!

Allison >> MESA, AZ >> USA

WHAT I WORE...

★ blouse Express
★ tie found
★ skirt handmade
★ thigh highs Express
★ shoes Target
★ petti Ebay

"By the table"

WHAT I WORE...

★ cardigan thrifted
★ dress Ebay
★ belt H&M
★ thick white tights and dinosaur necklace!

Katherine >> BURBANK, CA >> USA

"rainbow sherbet
on a sugar cone"

WHAT I WORE...

★ dress vintage from Aardvark's
★ knee socks sockdreams.com
★ shoes Seychelles from UO
★ earrings H&M
★ bracelet purchased at the farmer's
market by work

" Music "

WHAT I WORE...

★ jacket American Vintage
★ jeans Cheap Monday
★ shoes Zara

WHAT I WORE...

★ shirt vintage
★ jump suit asos.com
★ leggings Matalan
★ shoes Dunnes
★ necklace Mikey

"Party wardrobe"

WHAT I WORE...

cardigan Club Monaco (new but with lots
of little holes from my new kitten!)
belt with wooden buckle vintage
coach bag vintage
floral dress vintage
gladiator shoes vintage (my favorite shoes
from my favorite vintage store!)

"I've got the day off and the sun is shining!"

I WORE...

...or some reason i seem to wear yellow
...ll the time...
★ shirt H&M
★ skirt Primark
★ belt F21
★ headband somewhere in London
★ tights don't know

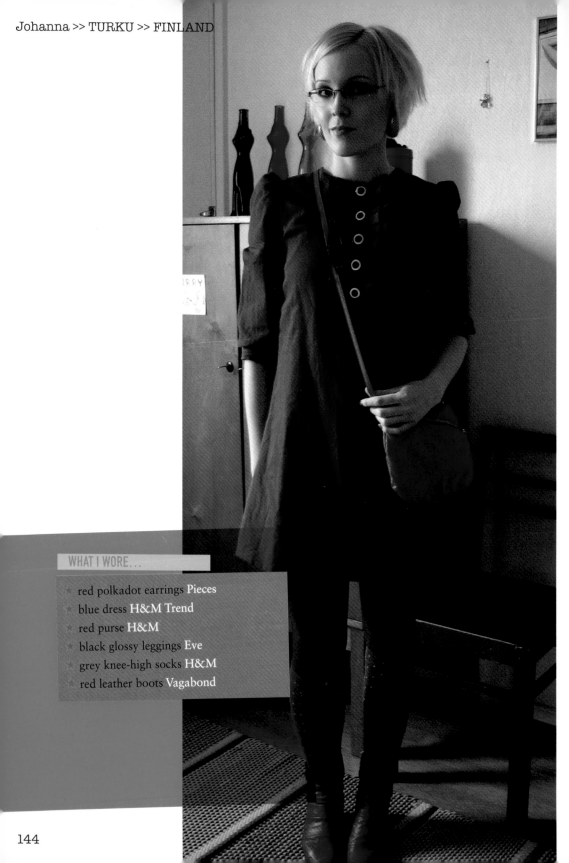

WHAT I WORE...

★ red polkadot earrings **Pieces**
★ blue dress **H&M Trend**
★ red purse **H&M**
★ black glossy leggings **Eve**
★ grey knee-high socks **H&M**
★ red leather boots **Vagabond**

WHAT I WORE...

★ everything was thrifted

"Anchors away!
It's absolutely
summery today!
I need a slurpee!"

WHAT I WORE…

★ 1950s navy chiffon petal hat
  with netting thrifted

★ kid's undershirt with lace details
  thrifted new

★ navy linen skirt with embroidery
  Anthropologie

★ vintage navy Clarks thrifted
  deadstock!

★ nautical scarf worn as belt
  thrifted

★ huge navy wooden bead necklace
  thrifted

★ orange glass head earrings made
  by me whiteapple.etsy.com

WHAT I WORE...

★ yellow ruffle dress thrifted
★ Minnetonka moccasins online
★ cowrie shell necklace thrifted

WHAT I WORE…

i ran out of socks today

★ sweater A&F
★ dress Anne Taylor Loft
★ skirt Gap
★ tights Macy's
★ boots Aldo

WHAT I WORE...

★ World Wildlife Fund tank JC Penney
★ skirt thrifted
★ penguin sneakers Kohl's
★ bracelet $1 Store

" Today was a day for pandas and pink penguins "

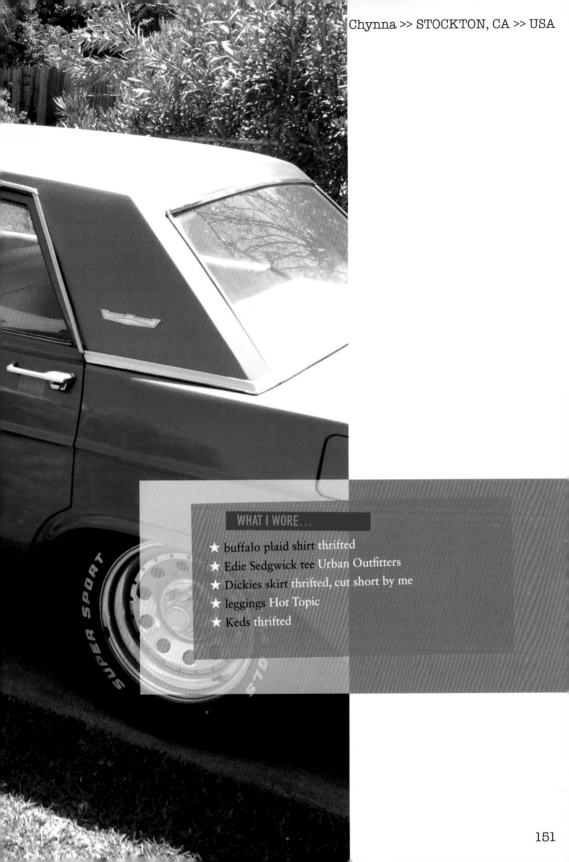

WHAT I WORE...

★ buffalo plaid shirt thrifted
★ Edie Sedgwick tee Urban Outfitters
★ Dickies skirt thrifted, cut short by me
★ leggings Hot Topic
★ Keds thrifted

Before my
art show
date

WHAT I WORE...

★ dress thrifted
★ black cami Victoria's
★ flats F21 clearance (one plus of having
   big feet...my size is always left!)
★ necklace and bracelet Brighton Hearts
★ ring F21
★ cheesy grin always

"Color blocks. Quick snap before I hit the church on a Sunday afternoon."

WHAT I WORE...

★ color blocks nu-rave tee
  hand-me-down from brother
★ men's black bow tie worn as
  wristband thrifted
★ high waist skinnies Lee Jeans

WHAT I WORE...

thrifted wolf tee
American Apparel skirt
vintage gray leather boots

WHAT I WORE...

★ necklace vintage, thrifted, amazing
★ dress Target
★ belt thrifted
★ shoes remixed, Steve Madden

WHAT I WORE...

★ leotard American Apparel
★ shorts Go International
★ flats Easy
★ necklace vintage

WHAT I WORE...

DDLE:

jeans second hand Ebay

"chucks" H&M kids

leather jacket H&M

cardigan H&M

top H&M

pullover Orsay

scarf handmade

BOTTOM:

★ pants H&M trend

★ tee H&M

★ scarf H&M

★ pendant Ebay

★ necklace vintage

★ tights vintage

★ shoes C&A

★ jacket New Sensation

WHAT I WORE...

hidden pockets

★ blouse $5 on sale at TJ Maxx

★ vest and tights H&M

★ skirt Lux, Urban Outfitters (i took it in at the waist and let out the hem about three inches)

★ belt and hat vintage, from my mom's antique and collectable shop (Hourgla Consignment in South Florida)

★ shoes Nine West

"Lion tamer."

WHAT I WORE...

★ dress H&M
★ hat Dillard's
★ necklace Ebay
★ socks Hue
★ boots Zappos
★ kitty ferocious

WHAT I WORE...

★ **dress** thrifted
★ **owl necklace** Girl Props
★ **beaded clutch** thrifted
★ **shoes** Kmart
★ **fake Raybans** gift from friend

"Happy birthday to me.
I'm officially a quarter of a century today. Tonight
a small group friends are going to my roomie's
cabin for the weekend in small town 'thrift heaven'
Minnesota. Yes!! Maybe the thrift gods will be nice
to me on my birthday..."

My eyes have grown allergic to contact lenses — I'm now perpetually in glasses. I think I look like a little bald owl in glasses with my hair tied up but oh well. "

WHAT I WORE...

preppy look
★ cardigan Fox
★ t-shirt Tangs
★ ribbon came with another skirt
★ belt Topshop
★ skirt Gap
★ socks River Island
★ shoes Ras (from Hue)
★ bag Converse

"Going to class makes me blue."

WHAT I WORE...

★ cardigan navy with hand-sewn button embellishments
★ knitted dress thrifted
★ leggings blue-dark purple (Forever New)
★ shoes black flats with red wooden block (Novo)

WHAT I WORE...

tank Target
pencil skirt Goodwill by the pound
belt Goodwill by the pound
shoes Ebay
necklace Ebay

"Determined not to let work stifle my wardrobe fun. I wore this to fill out all my new hire paperwork at the library and subtracted the necklace and cardi and added the belt when I got home.

"Inspiration: girls at London fashion week with orange tights."

WHAT I WORE...

this one goes out to Kumar...thanks for the shirt!

★ **80s Garfield shirt** from Kumar

★ **grey wool skirt** thrifted yesterday

★ **belt** Salvation Army

★ **feather headband** antique store in IL

★ **tights** Target

★ **t-straps** Jeffrey Campbell

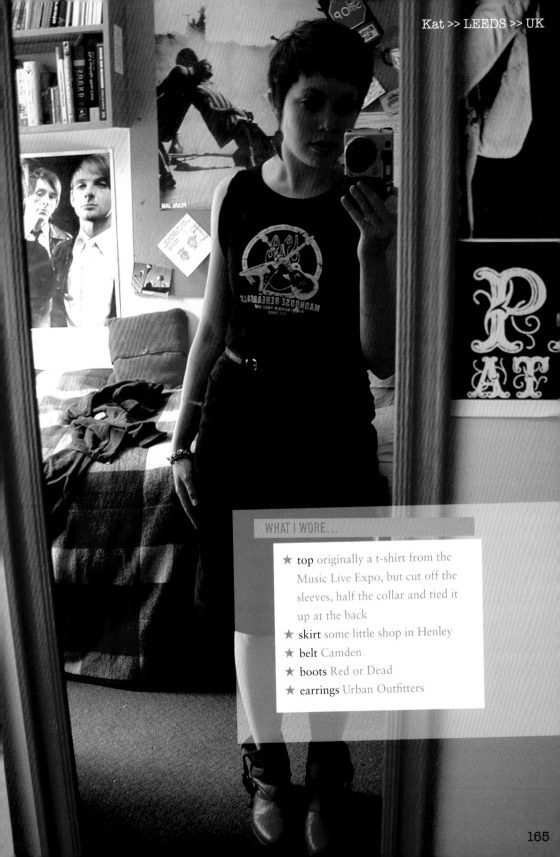

WHAT I WORE...

★ **top** originally a t-shirt from the
Music Live Expo, but cut off the
sleeves, half the collar and tied it
up at the back
★ **skirt** some little shop in Henley
★ **belt** Camden
★ **boots** Red or Dead
★ **earrings** Urban Outfitters

WHAT I WORE...

- ★ green cardigan some outlet store
- ★ blue dress thrifted
- ★ purple tights cut
- ★ socks possibly stolen from siblings
- ★ necklace thrifted

"It was only -10 out today so I celebrated by not wearing pants out!"

WHAT I WORE...

★ **western shirt** it was my dad's from th
70s, it is Levi's brand
★ **cardigan** Gap
★ **jeans** Forever 21
★ **boots** thrift
★ **chain purse** thrift

WHAT I WORE…

★ beanie stole from a friend!
★ orange necklace Senegal
★ kids denim jacket thrifted
★ white tank don't know
★ yellow top H&M Amsterdam
★ jeans gift from sis…no brand, but i
   LOVE them!
★ sandals Payless

"**Instead of studying I decided to play dress up**

WHAT I WORE...

★ this is one of my favorite dresses, the sailor dress! I love the colored buttons at the side :)

★ yellow stockings are one of my favorite too!

The lighting is horrible in the room in which this picture was taken. I played around with settings to lighten it a little, but it still is not quite right.

WHAT I WORE...

★ loafers Value Village
★ nylons Walgreens
★ navy blue skirt Goodwill
★ belt Goodwill
★ shirt Urban Outfitters
★ dark brown sweater H&M
★ bracelet (hard to see) Luther North thrift shop (Addison and Austin, Chicago)

WHAT I WORE...

TOP: trying on my new lamé leggings :-)
★ sweater Urban Outfitters
★ miniskirt hand-made
★ leggings American Apparel
★ shoes Irregular Choice

BOTTOM:
★ coat Pinko
★ green jeans local store
★ booties Sugar
★ bag Scout
★ brooch H&M

"I'm back...and today it's officially fall.
Rainy-windy-cold day!"

"This came all the way from London.

Stupid Gap got taken away from the stupid Metrocenter so when I went to London I raided the stupid Gap there. Stupid really."

WHAT I WORE...

★ yum@all in one. as you may have guessed it was from Gap

★ the scarf's from my mum's wardrobe

★ and the white t-shirt is one of the several million I have

WHAT I WORE…

chilly day
★ shirt AE
★ hat vintage
★ jeans can't remember
★ shoes Nine West
★ socks my sister's closet

"Got polka?"

WHAT I WORE...

cheating on my regime, Oh O!
- ★ jeans gift from sister
- ★ top local market
- ★ shoes Tex
- ★ belt little sister's
- ★ earrings sister's
- ★ hat on plastic head my dad's :)

BOTTOM: Bryan calls this the A.D.D. chair. i'm actually at an Anthropologie store in Santana Row in San Jose.

"I had that dream again.

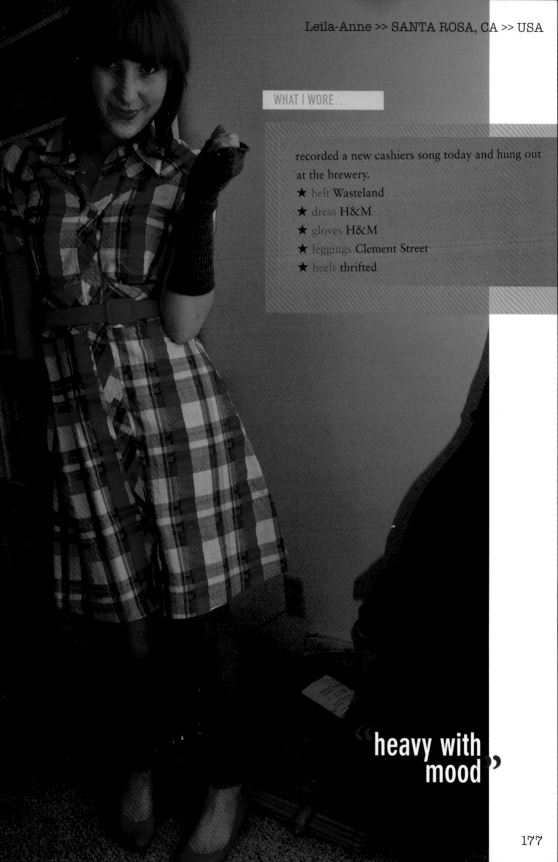

WHAT I WORE...

recorded a new cashiers song today and hung out at the brewery.

★ belt Wasteland
★ dress H&M
★ gloves H&M
★ leggings Clement Street
★ heels thrifted

"heavy with mood"

WHAT I WORE...

now i need a yellow onesie to match
MY bike
★ onesie H&M
★ shoes Clarks
★ bike Iro Angus (not mine)

WHAT I WORE...

heart sunnies
★ **sunglasses** Fred Flare
★ **dress** forgot where i got it
★ **shoes** bought in Shanghai
★ i dyed my **white tights** last weekend. i
think i need to dye it some more.

179

JE T'AIME

JE T'AIME

WHAT I WORE...

★ headband Victor & Rolf
★ blouse Gap
★ pants Gap
★ belt American Apparel
★ shoes Chloé
★ watch Marc Jacobs

"I woke up with a headache and it is crazy raining out today. I have not time for this!

WHAT I WORE...

★ piggy sweatshirt thrifted
★ jeans mall store
★ Chucks

"Just got off of a red-eye flight and decided to wear something as close to a nightgown as possible."

WHAT I WORE...

★ Libertine for Target purple ticking shirt-
dress with white bib detail
★ gray cable tights from H&M
★ red cutout t-strap flats by Mariana
by GOLC
★ feeling:
cute: 4
functional: 5
creative: 1 (too tired to do anything!!)

WHAT I WORE...

★ lace blouse, boots Kohl's
★ jeans Gordmans

WHAT I WORE...

★ pink tights Marks and Spencer
★ blue denim dress Bang Bang on Berwick Stre
  (it's a clothing exchange shop)
★ lime green cardigan H&M, bought when i w
  still in 6th form!
★ blue and white stripy top C&A in Zurich (w
  so excited to see C&A again!)

WHAT I WORE...

hoes Camper
ghts mystery! they're a few years old and
ve been around
umper maybe Kohl's?
acket thrifted
hirt Walmart?
ed head

Sunshine for
Autumn "

WHAT I WORE...

★ shirt Guess
★ black tank can't remember
★ braces costume shop
★ wide leg pants Living Doll
★ boots Wittner
★ brooch Etsy, Red Are The Roses

WHAT I WORE...

★ shirt H&M
★ skirt thrifted
★ tights thrifted
★ knee socks H&M
★ belt thrifted
★ scarf my grandmother's
★ beret thrifted
★ necklace my grandmother's
★ shoes thrifted

WHAT I WORE...

★ white/silver scarf thrifted a while back
★ vintage lightning bolt earrings thrifted
★ dragonfly pendant thrifted
★ vintage plum frock thrifted (have you ever used the last cash in your wallet to buy one thing at the thrift store? i have...)
★ gold etched bangle flea market
★ white leather tote thrifted at a majorly huge Salvation Army in the northern suburbs
★ friendship bracelet belt thrifted
★ clear wedge jellies with toe cut out swapped from Ivy Frozen

WHAT I WORE...

i just organized a space
★ limited edition doors tee Ebay
★ 90s denim skirt remixed
★ Ferragamos remixed

perb Hero! HAHAHAH!
I come to save
the world.**"**

WHAT I WORE...

OP:
★ two-tone neon tee dress Project Edit
★ fabric prints bag Pumpkin Pie
★ thrifted yellow flips
★ bubble soap pink robot Union mall marke

BOTTOM: sweetie candy
★ neon evil cat tee from Jatujak weekend market
★ high waist neon pink pencil skirt The Old Story
★ vinyl two-tone loose bag Heidi's Secrets
★ turquoise pumps from Ratchada night market
★ neon green, blue stripes toy watch Lego

191

WHAT I WORE...

★ skirt vintage
★ belt vintage
★ ankle boots vintage
★ tank American Apparel tri-blend
★ sunglasses vintage Givenchy

WHAT I WORE...

★ purple top from local mall
★ yellow high waisted skirt from local market pour 3 Euros
★ flats local market
★ clutch Windsor store
★ flower headband local store
★ pink nail polish local market goodies :)

WHAT I WORE…

★ lace top Western Gear shop
★ shorts old jeans i cut
★ jazz shoes thrifted
★ chiffon scarf flea market
★ vinyl bag found it in my barn
★ vintage sunglasses my mom's

WHAT I WORE...

★ finding this faux fur hat a real staple right now, and it doesn't give me hat head either

★ sale jumper romper H&M

★ boots Aldo

★ feather and fan cowl: knit by me: yarnovermovement.etsy.com

WHAT I WORE...

★ coat from Ebay store, Thriftwares
★ shoes Steve Madden
★ bag J. Crew
★ dress Zara

"**Please excuse my scowl
I think the sun was in my eyes
>:(**"

WHAT I WORE...

TOP: ★ denim jacket from Taiwan
★ tank Zara
★ skirt AA
★ flats vintage

BOTTOM: today, i went adventuring in my
basement. and lo and behold i found the most
perfect shirt ever. it belongs to my granma. it's
pink and gold, with golden rings. i wore
it with pride.
★ shirt vintage from grammy
★ Hello Kitty necklace self-made
★ shorts Urban Outfitters
★ footless tights H&M
★ flats Gap
★ ring Anna Sui (contains lipgloss as well!)
★ bracelets many places

Leila-Anne >> SANTA ROSA, CA >> USA

WHAT I WORE...

★ top **Old Navy**
★ belt **H&M**
★ skirt **Buffalo Exchange (by Diesel)**
★ shoes **thrifted in Portland (Stuart Weitzman!)**
★ earrings **H&M**
★ bracelet **Clement Street**

WHAT I WORE...

★ blouse F21
★ jeans Levi's
★ heeled oxfords Zinda

"Major heatwave! It was
90+ degrees today."

WHAT I WORE...

★ huge specs Tekka mall
★ shirt threadless.com
★ high-waisted shorts Mango

"And the night has come.
My sister took this after I came back from dinner,
what yummy food. Okay, school has started and it's
really exciting. So sorry that I've not been loading that
much photos as my schedule is quite busy .But I'll be
posting more really soon!"

WHAT I WORE...

e the foldover edge on this cardigan, it also has great
re pockets, i got it about a month ago
laid cardigan vintage

"Hank's Angels" t-shirt my uncle screenprinted these
-shirts in the 70s for a bunch of the girls in the town
ve grew up in. i think it's supposed to be a play on
vords with "Hell's Angels"

ilver cassette necklace although you can't really see
t, it's a beautiful silver necklace, made from a hand
culpted mold of a tiny cassette tape, made by my friend
laine. her company is called Roadkill, check it out

grey jeans my own design for the company i work for

lack boots Office in London

WHAT I WORE...

TOP and BOTTOM: ★ ridiculous sunglasses!
★ green striped dress vintage, from a shop on Valencia in SF
★ black leggings
★ Alexandre Herchcovitch for Melissa wedges
★ WWII Belgian satchel

MIDDLE: ★ pink sparkle knit hat
★ turquoise and gold vintage dress
★ poodle bag (!!!) from Love On A Leash
★ rings by Tarina Tarantino
★ pink high heels from Patricia Field

WHAT I WORE...

★ black and white dress Oliver Bonas
★ pink tights Marks and Spencer
★ black shoes a tiny shop in Hockley in Nottingham (Steph's, she's had them since first year uni)
★ Bird on hairband Broadway Market

WHAT I WORE...

★ a Las Vegas tank
★ skirt my sis'
★ tube bag Jacques Ruc
★ ice cream from Nadia :]

mi salón de colorines

WHAT I WORE...

starting from the top:
★ yellow scarf free from a friend
★ lace and striped cami Target
★ vintage sunglasses Laurel Thrift
★ black and white striped screenprinted t-shirt
   the Gap
★ blue tunic cardigan Target
★ vintage woven leather belt Laurel Thrift
★ skinny jeans Volcom
★ light brown boots Payless (unseen)

Anthropologie meets Alice in Wonderland.

WHAT I WORE...

★ dress Anthropologie
★ tights target
★ shoes Nordstrom Rack
★ headband Urban Outfitters
★ gloves vintage, yard sale
★ crazy walls my unfinished kitchen

WHAT I WORE…

★ a vintage brown jacquard dress
★ hot pink tights Target
★ vintage scarf
★ and black Fornarina maryjane heels

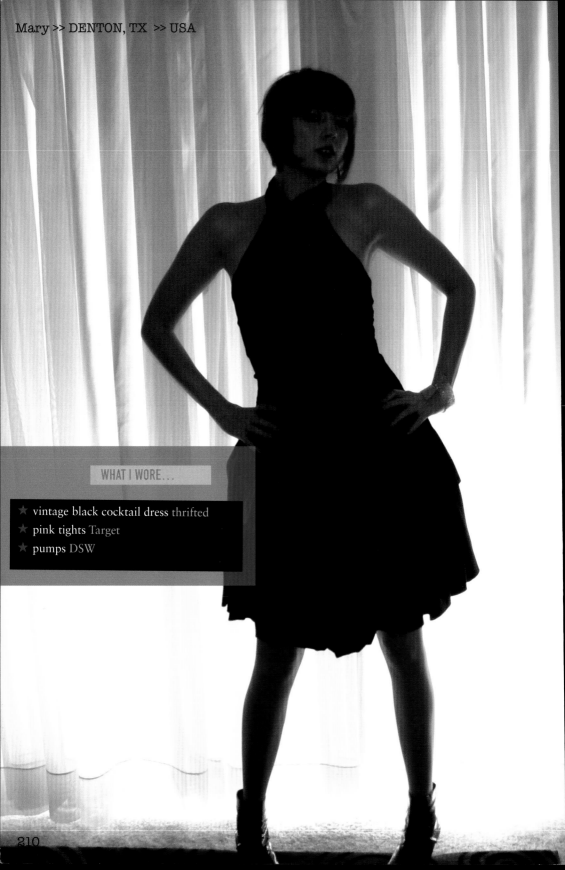

WHAT I WORE...

★ vintage black cocktail dress thrifted
★ pink tights Target
★ pumps DSW

WHAT I WORE...

★ shirt Pete vs. Toby
★ shorts H&M
★ leggings Steed Lord for H&M
★ sneakers Blowfish

Down under

WHAT I WORE...

★ red shoes H&M
★ black trousers a local clothes store
★ red shirt bought years ago
★ white shirt H&M (Fashion
   against Aids)
★ red sweater borrowed from my mom
★ necklace gift from my boyfriend

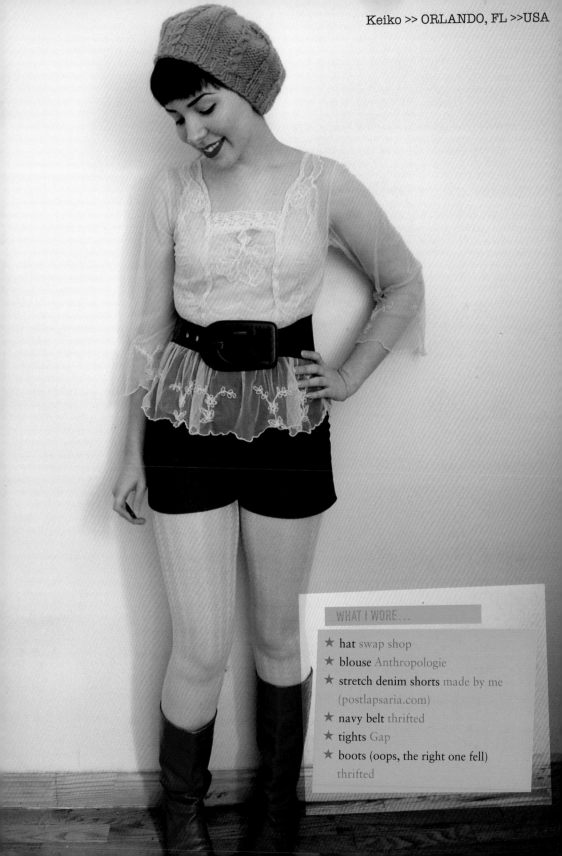

WHAT I WORE...

★ hat swap shop
★ blouse Anthropologie
★ stretch denim shorts made by me
   (postlapsaria.com)
★ navy belt thrifted
★ tights Gap
★ boots (oops, the right one fell)
   thrifted

"Beautiful sunny weather today. But I am a careful and distrustful person, hence the scarf."

WHAT I WORE...

★ **scarf** found in my mother's closet (s
   won it at a charity raffle/tombola, i
   think)
★ **shirt** Review
★ **cardigan** Montego
★ **pants** H&M
★ **shoes** Puma

WHAT I WORE...

to Starbucks
★ hybrid chain beaded necklace made
   by Ru
★ red flower shirt Mono+ (a very
   comfortable gift from my cousin)
★ black bubble piece Kosit
★ black beaded slippers Bus Stop
★ green tote gift from P (trip to
   Cambodia i think)

WHAT I WORE...

★ coat China
★ blue mesh top Valleygirl
★ pink singlet Cotton On
★ secondhand purple skirt (it looks
   hand-made)
★ black tights
★ boots from Target

WHAT I WORE...

★ **dress** New York, think it was Zara or some
  other high street shop.
★ **bangles** Accessorize
★ **shoes** borrowed from Helen (from Schuh)
★ **beads** Helen's (M&S)
★ **cardigan** Jane Norman

WHAT I WORE...

TOP:
- ★ dress Kookai
- ★ belt Sportsgirl from 14 years ago!
- ★ trio of Dinosaur Design bangles
- ★ green beads Rozelle Markets
- ★ wedges store in Bondi some years ago (i have not worn them in ages)
- ★ blue oversized sunnies Grandma Takes a Trip in Bondi
- ★ wig bought at The Costume Shop in Surry Hills (while my car was getting washed! heehee)

MIDDLE: i have not indulged in ANY form of retail therapy for a very looooong time and again today almost passed up the opportunity to break the spell... universal forces thought otherwise and soon i was saying hi to Rosie (she used to serve up my coffee at Bertoni's!) and perusing the "goods"! :)
at first nothing...but gradually i warmed to the sport, an ol' favourite and away i went albeit still cautiously... only very special, unusual and quality...otherwise one ends up with waaaayyyy too many things

- ★ anyway, this dress was a last-minute spot and at $12.50, inexpensive, whimsical and fancy-free (AND a tad cheeky to boot!)
- ★ peacock necklace Rozelle Markets
- ★ pincushion pendant necklace (self-made) pendant from St.Vinnies in Gosford

BOTTOM: heading off to Forster for the weekend...
- ★ smock store at EQ
- ★ grey cardi JeansWest Erina
- ★ purple tights Equip Erina
- ★ ankle-tie flats Novo Erina
- ★ leather flower with brooch St Vinnies Rozelle
- ★ bag Salvos
- ★ purple perspex bangle Bondi Markets
- ★ pink polish Chanel

219

WHAT I WORE...

★ hat Urban Outfitters
★ dress Topshop
★ brooch (on dress) vintage fur brooch from a
  antique store.
★ purse thrifted
★ tights H&M
★ shoes Zara

A hint of Little Red
Riding Hood.

WHAT I WORE...

★ cardigan Promod
★ dress from the X-dream store
★ brooch market in Shanghai
★ knee-high socks Gina Tricot
★ boots Vagabond

"My new favorite shirt by fello
Nemo graphic designer And
who also runs Tribut
Skateboards. I'm proud to be
Portland People Eater, whateve
that means

WHAT I WORE...

★ shirt Tribute Skateboards
★ striped long-sleeved shirt Gap
★ knit beret F21
★ jeans Levi's
★ belt Wild & Lethal Trash
★ heeled oxfords Made By Elves

WHAT I WORE...

ike to match my furniture :)

kissing birdie necklace New Orleans

1950s Blue Roses Dress Eugene, OR

robin's egg blue gloves

white sunglasses

white strappy shoes

i've never wished so hard for peacock

blue stockings!

WHAT I WORE...

chilly day
★ shirt AE
★ hat vintage
★ jeans don't know
★ shoes Nine West
★ socks my sister's closet

WHAT I WORE…

TOP: library and class
★ headband H&M
★ necklace thrifted
★ black turtleneck thrifted, remixed infinity times
★ jungle green/aqua top Old Navy
★ belt Grandma
★ skirt thrifted

MIDDLE: ★ headband H&M
★ scarf gift from grandma
★ cardigan Target
★ giraffe brooch flea market
★ aqua dress thrifted and hemmed shorter
★ knee socks Target
★ bangle Forever 21
★ shoes thrifted (Nine West, they look brand new)

BOTTOM: i do think i look a bit like old nobility, or perhaps as if i am about to seek mischief on the high seas? not that they are mutually exclusive.
★ shades Target
★ white scarf thrifted
★ brooch on knot of scarf H&M
★ black cardigan Old Navy
★ belt from my Grandma
★ red tee Urban Outfitters
★ blue skirt thrifted

"Aristocratic pirate"

WHAT I WORE...

my skirt looks red, but it's really a burnt orange

★ earrings thrifted
★ top thrifted, by Banana Republic
★ belt thrifted from Fukijai Market in Senegal an
   held together by safety pins
★ vintage skirt thrifted
★ gold sandals thrifted

WHAT I WORE...

★ gray sweater vintage
★ cloud brooch indie designer in HK
★ white longsleeved top Urban Outfitters
★ white pleated skirt clothing swap
★ black bodysuit American Apparel
★ socks vintage deadstock
★ boots bought in HK

Just figuring out the timer/placing the camera thing. That's why I'm off to the side. Let's call it "artsy"

"Tall in heels"

WHAT I WORE...

★ **blouse** Morgan de Toi bargain from local market
★ **jeans** Paris Blues
★ **striped heels** local market
★ **earrings** mom's :)

WHAT I WORE...

green dress
orange footless tights
teal bag
dark green t-strap shoes
accessories

WHAT I WORE...

★ frilly shirt found at a random festival
★ Body Line jacket
★ Riachuelo shorts and hairbow
★ hand made necklace
   Montreal rocking horse shoes
   Body Line and Lupo socks and tights
   Body Line bag
   pin given to me by Meh
   random belt with a heart buckle
   given to me by Lily
   VW replica/Le Café/hand-made rings
   featuring Gloomy

GUAR dress: how I
rned 30 freakin 5!
o tomorrow is my
tual 35th birthday,
my family is taking
me out to the San
ancisco yacht club
inner tonight. And
s full of stuffy rich
es, so I thought I'd
t my fierce Jaguar
ess — because I'm
ious that way! I've
d it for nearly two
rs, but have never
worn it out. "

WHAT I WORE...

★ JAGUAR dress from La Meow Vintage
★ cardigan H&M
★ black belt F21
★ gray tee American Apparel
★ 80s pumps thrifted
★ pink clutch F21

231

"Don't mind my dog Guy, he loves getting in the way of photos."

WHAT I WORE...

i completely forgot about this top, i bought it for two dollars at the Gap outlet in early winter.

★ tunic Gap outlet
★ jeans Forever 21
★ boots thrifted
★ chain purse thrifted

HAT I WORE…

OP: superhero zebra inside. you need to
watch Iron Man.

- @ncestor black and white striped dress
  with (another) statement bib
- Zara black tights
- DMK black oxford lace-up heels
- Bata bag
- Vivie plastic spectacles
- vintage red earrings with gold stripes
- MNG black and white striped plastic
  bangles
- Livia blue plastic bangle
- Diva red faux skin bangle

OP: i am a wee upset because one of
e straps on this bag (one of my all-time
ve and from past comments, seems to be
urs too) is tearing apart. gah. it is held
tact by the stitching but i think it might
ve way soon…

- @ncestor blue glittery cardigan
- @ncestor red geometric dress
- Cotton On gray tights
- Zara multi-colored patchwork tote
- gold shoes from FEP
- vintage gold earrings with diamantes
- Diva gold dragonfly necklace
- Cotton On red wooden bangle
- My Room wooden bangles with gold
  studs
- vintage white bangle with gold stars
- vintage gold bangle
- assorted gold bangles
- Paul Frank calculator watch

**" Monday Blues (and red
and gray and gold and
rainbow. So, blues? No,
not really) "**

WHAT I WORE...

★ jacket Macy's
★ skirt (worn as dress) thrifted
★ leggings gift from Mom
★ shoes Dillard's
★ jewelry thrifted

"The jacket is from Macy's. When I worked there, I saved all my "employee bucks" and eventually, the stars (and sales) aligned and I ended up getting this $70 jacket for about $15 or so."

idn't want my beehive to get
wet so I wore this awesome
arf. I felt so colorful and like
movie star. In technicolor :)"

WHAT I WORE…

scarf thrifted

coat thrifted

skirt thrfited

blouse thrifted

tights and shoes Target

WHAT I WORE...

★ **dress** estate sale (yes, my famous
   yellow belt came with it!)
★ **shoes** thrifted (by Jante)

WHAT I WORE...

earrings handmade
scarf Mrs. Hippie
cardigan EDC
b+w brooch vintage
gray shirt old turtleneck i cut off
red skirt H&M
tights don't remember
flats Vagabond

Inspiration: all those cute Finnish girls with their big, big tops and small, short bottoms.

WHAT I WORE...

★ **dress** thrifted
★ **shoes** thrifted
★ **sweater** gift

WHAT I WORE...

crochet-sleeve tee Old Navy
pocket skirt American Apparel
black oxfords

"Are knee socks allowed in the Spring? I wanted to wear my black slouchy socks, but I could only find one!"

239

WHAT I WORE...

★ green puff skirt thrifted
★ turtle neck stirrup bodysuit new
  deadstock thrifted
★ black leather jacket thrifted
★ black high heel ankle booties thrifted

" I found this cute late 80's/early 90s skirt by Cristina. I remember going to the Cristina store in the mall with my older teen relatives and thinking how I loved the clothes. This skirt comes to a point at the waist, puffs out and has a emblem on the side!

WHAT I WORE...

★ cardigan Target
★ striped dress thrifted
★ pink slip Victoria's Secret
★ gray knee highs Urban Outfitters
★ black boots thrifted

TOP: didn't bother moving the Tide box. this is my fave dress of the moment...i've been saving it for a long time. but now the time is right :D
★ dress work, $15
★ belt remixed, random thrift
★ cardi remixed, yet again :P, Gap
★ tank work, $10
★ necklace remixed, thrifted

MIDDLE: the concert last night was awesome: D. too bad i have to work today =(
★ tee work, $10
★ skirt remixed, random thrift
★ vest $4, VV
★ belt remixed, VV
★ shoes Gap, $13
★ bows Shoe Clips, $2, Value Village
★ necklace remixed, H&M
★ headband $3, H&M

BOTTOM: melt my heart to stone...YAYAY this is the debut of two of my many thrifted finds from my week of awesome-thriftedness two weeks ago.
★ blazer $4, thrifted. when i found this, my friend Emily and i had been talking about how badly we wanted a classic blazer with gold buttons. lo and behold, i found one! and it was half price :D
★ tank $7, work
★ skirt $4, MCC (a thrift store), also found in my awesome-thriftedness!
★ moccasins remixed, thrifted
★ necklace remixed, work
★ flats remixed, Old Navy

AT I WORE…

- earrings handmade
- scarf tied in a bow from swap with *franca*
- old gray shirt
- blue cardigan, brown boots Esprit
- bangle from mum
- dress worn as skirt Blutsgeschwister
- black tights
- black legwarmers H&M

WHAT I WORE...

★ secondhand bag and dress and belt
★ shoes a market in Broome

"Wearing my summery skirt
as a dress again...
its been way too hot."

WHAT I WORE…

★ hat NY Hat Co
★ top thrifted
★ cardigan Zara
★ jacket H&M
★ jeans Cheap Monday
★ belt mum's old
★ shoes Bianco

" Going to the teaparty. "

WHAT I WORE...

TOP: and later, to Cirque du Soleil.
★ everything is either hand made or off brand
★ except for Meta bloomers

BOTTOM:
★ alice bow Body Line
★ shirt Anna House
★ skirt Body Line
★ handbag JUNKS
★ socks Puket w/ hand made toppers
★ shoes Montreal
★ parasol Meta
★ rings Vivienne Westwood, Claire's, Anatoonstore
★ necklace Anatoonstore
★ earrings Japanese Candy
★ bloomers you can't see Swimmer
★ petti you can't see handmade
★ keyrings on the bag San X/ H.Naoto/ off brand

WHAT I WORE...

TOP: i look so cranky... my sister was taking f
to take this photo... at least the yard looks gre
★ red cardigan thrifted
★ black shirt Sportsgirl
★ lavender beads thrifted
★ royal blue dress thrifted (it actually has a c
  Hawaiian-y print that you can't really see)
★ tights plucked from the masses, probs Cole
★ lavender Cons General Pants (unseen)

MIDDLE:
★ shoes kids section of Target amazing they fit ever
though I'm a size 8!
★ tights forget, probably Coles or something
★ dress vintage, it's really nice lace
★ net belt vintage
★ floral singlet made by me!
★ chain with bow chain from Target and bow is a
  shoe clip
★ inspiration it's nearly spring here! also a little bit
  Alice in Wonderland

BOTTOM: floral blue birds
★ blue shoes thrifted, Salvo's $4
★ tights can't remember
★ floral shirt dress thrifted, customized
★ black swing jacket thrifted, customized
★ red singlet Kmart
★ bird pin my mum's
★ inspiration spring (again!) and my all
  encompassing passion for ridiculous florals

WHAT I WORE...

★ red bow handmade
★ red puff-sleeved shift dress H&M
★ navy belt Savers
★ navy tights Walmart
★ white boots Wet Seal

"tea parties and bridge playing"

WHAT I WORE...

★ free tights from friend
★ thrifted dress
★ thrifted belt
★ thrifted shoes
★ my pup's stuffed giraffe

WHAT I WORE...

m in Rzeszów visiting my parents for a
w days but this photo was made at my
oyfriend's home, i was going to meet my
iend

★ red turtleneck sweater Pull & Bear
★ t-shirt second hand George
★ shorts H&M
★ black tights Calzedonia
★ leg warmers H&M
★ boots second hand
★ bag Cropp

WHAT I WORE...

very comfortable!!
★ hoodie Fila by Lillywhites
★ shirt H&M
★ shorts Freesoul
★ shoes Vans
★ socks American Apparel
★ bag local store
★ scarf local store

WHAT I WORE...

yeah, finally i have the time to post an outfit. i promise i'll do it more often

★ **shirt** threadless.com
★ **skirt** vintage, thrifted (Salvation Army)
★ **belt** vintage, mom's
★ **leggings** some store, can't recall
★ **bangles** Forever 21, Black Clover etc

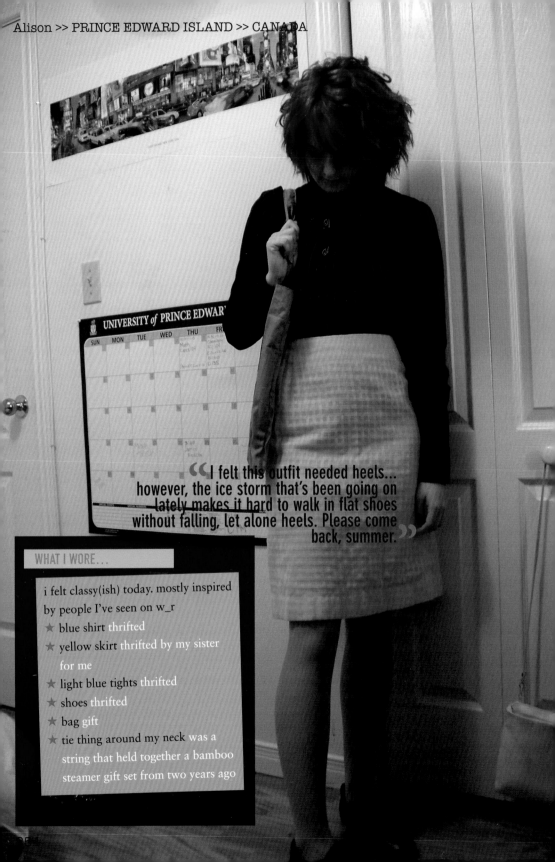

UNIVERSITY of PRINCE EDWAR'

SUN   MON   TUE   WED   THU   FR

"I felt this outfit needed heels...
however, the ice storm that's been going on
lately makes it hard to walk in flat shoes
without falling, let alone heels. Please come
back, summer."

WHAT I WORE...

i felt classy(ish) today. mostly inspired
by people I've seen on w_r
★ blue shirt thrifted
★ yellow skirt thrifted by my sister
   for me
★ light blue tights thrifted
★ shoes thrifted
★ bag gift
★ tie thing around my neck was a
   string that held together a bamboo
   steamer gift set from two years ago

"My friend Frances called me ridiculous for saying this shirt was 'Proustian'"

WHAT I WORE...

★ "Proust" shirt Topshop
★ ribbon is of course random
★ good old leather bag Topshop
★ watch Ted Baker
★ jeans Only
★ purple patent shoes Next

WHAT I WORE...

6th Ave! navy and black = one of
all time best color combos ever!

★ black checked button-down
vintage

★ navy pencil skirt vintage

★ little boy's black blazer vintage

★ Mexican belt vintage

★ black watch from my mom!

★ BCBG Max Azria rafia wedges

"Ha ha...yesterday we went to a club in town. It's small but we could drink as many cocktails as possible for free until 12 p.m. But the girls always look the same there...

WHAT I WORE...

★ **dress** QS by S.Oliver
★ **skirt** vintage
★ **tights** Ernstings Family
★ **shoes** Deichmann
★ **necklace** H&M

"I met up with the most lovely irene_adler yesterday! It was so great to meet her and believe me, she really is at least as sweet in person as you can imagine! I was wearing this jacket yesterday too and it turned out that she had thrifted this earlier and then sold it to someone on Finnish online auction site huuto.net because it was too big for her. Last week I bought this jacket from that someone without knowing that it originally belonged to irene_adler :-) What a delightful coincidence!

WHAT I WORE...

★ scarf H&M
★ vintage 60s jacket (grey/pink check) second hand from online auction site huuto.net, originally thrifted by irene_adler
★ gloves Aleksi 13, 50% sale
★ stripy dress vintage, Ebay
★ shoes Bianco
★ eyeglasses YSL

WHAT I WORE...

TOP: oh, that naive smile...
- aqua Conversey knock-offs, JC Penney (for $3! I had a friend working in the shoe department and he kept his eyes open for me)
- shorts Target
- blue tank Target
- black tank Old Navy
- flats remixed, Old Navy

TOP MIDDLE:
★ Elvis t-shirt Target
★ vest my mother's a looooong time ago
★ jeans Se7en (FREE! I still can't over that!)
★ Converses
★ the books: The Discarded Image (by C.S. Lewis), The Western Canon (by Harold Bloom), The Divine Comedy (by Dante), East of Eden (by John Steinbeck), and The Mind of the Maker (by Dorothy Sayers). i don't know why I start this many books at once.

BOTTOM MIDDLE:
- shoes Converse (bought them in 8th grade... they're starting to wear a bit thin)
- jeans Se7en
- blue shirt hand me down from my tiny great-aunt
- black tank Old Navy
- glasses Target (reading glasses!)

BOTTOM: kinda nerdy/shy chic...
- orangey-red shirt Old Navy
- blue wrap skirt Gap
- argyle socks Target
- Cons 8th grade
- pasty white legs Finals!!!

WHAT I WORE...

all of these things were cast aside by someone, but have since had a long and varied life with me – reworn and remixed in many ways, in many places, but never, ever together before. and almost surely, never ever together again

★ **70s men's shirt** is from that big secondhand place in SF, on Haight St...oh you know the one...i've been trying to remember the name of it...

★ **80s Esprit sweatshirt** i found in the street (ok, trash) in Brooklyn

★ **the skirt** (50s? it was a dress i cut, i think there was a bolero too) i got it at a flea market in Prague in 1996!! i wore it all the time thru the rest of the millennium and since then it's had more than one extended hiatus. i will never stop loving the pattern so it's hard for me to part with it even tho it's disintegrating

★ **bloomers** thrifted, are from the 60s? 70s? i'm having a hard time imagining their original purpose. why not a just regular slip? for warmth? for modesty? sleepwear? for culottes? probably culottes

★ **blue pinstriped tights** thrifted, i cut the feet off long ago b/c too short

★ **thigh high argyle tights** i thrifted in the 90s

★ **Enzo Anglioni gray suede shoes** thrifted brand-new a few years ago and worn often. <3

when i went out i also wore my:

★ **periwinkle scarf** found

★ **leather bag** that i use all the time thrifted

★ **super-warm down duvet-like coat** Filene's Basement? or something like that. when people hug me when i'm wearing it they want to settle in for a nap

if you just read all of this you might be ready for a nap too

WHAT I WORE...

★ **star earrings** thrift
★ **necklace** made from an old
   earring for my grandma
★ **cardigan** target
★ **belt** thrift
★ **shirt** blackheartbunny.com
★ **pants** very, very old pants
   (maybe 10 years?) originally
   purchased from a thrift store
   so they are really a piece of
   work at this point
★ **boots** thrift
★ **tights** drug store
★ **dog** cute and helpful

WHAT I WORE...

dress Anthropologie
apron birthday present from
graygoosie
shoes Miz Mooz
watch bracelet xmas gift from
my mil

WHAT I WORE...

TOP: jumpsuit for the lounging lady
★ jumpsuit vintage
★ shoes vintage Yves Saint Laurent these were my aunt's and she had never worn them!!

MIDDLE:
★ dress thrifted from Lost and Found markets, it has the sweetest little lambs printed on it!!
★ long sleeve top Metalicus
★ tights Ambre
★ shoes Sempre di By Biviel
★ gloves thrifted
★ belt don't remember
★ necklace thrifted

BOTTOM:
★ dress Ebay i woke myself up at 5am in the morning to bid on this! it was totally worth it!
★ tights Ambre
★ shoes Sempre di By Biviel i wear these shoes to death, they have to be the most comfortable heels i have ever bought! i put it down to the thickness of the heel!

WHAT I WORE...

★ **fur coat** hand me down
★ **scarf** thrifted
★ **tights** GTM
★ **shoes** sister's old shoes

"I felt like a little Russian orphan child all day."

Splatters Matter.

WHAT I WORE...

★ sunglasses Beacon's Closet
★ necklace vintage
★ cardigan Ann Taylor
★ sherbert tube top Arden B (thifted)
★ high waisted shorts Emanuel Ungaro
  (thifted)
★ holey jelly flats shoe market (in
  Brooklyn)
★ bag Hobo International

WHAT I WORE...

TOP: summer fling in white
i eventually went with a dark blue belt
of my mom's
a pashmina which is my mom's also he he
i didn't use the bag pictured here, instead i
brought my green weaved bag
i also use a necklace which i forgot where
i got that
i just bought the tube bag that day and it was
only Rp 139.000 (around US$14)

MIDDLE:
scarf Mangdu
dress Chic Simple
shorts Bugis
cardigan Mangdu
Rilakuma bag Some shop @ Gading
star badge Kipling's

BOTTOM:
white tee Bali
tube dress Gaudi
shorts Bugis
black flat shoes Singapore
Sesame Street school bus bag Michelle
blue belt from sister's dress
roll cake necklace from phone's strap

CREDITS AND CONTACT DETAILS

Graffito Books would like to extend huge thanks to all of the fantastic, creative people who have contributed images to the book.

If you would like to submit photographs for inclusion in the next edition please email us at info@graffitobooks.com

★ p4 Johanna Öst > johannaost. com / Madison Hartley > virginia-blue.blogspot.com > ebay:virginiabluevintage / Vlada > flickr.com/photos/go_i_know_not_wither_bring_back_i_know_not_what / Michelle Lam > flickr: Avarine

★ p5 Hannah Hundley > flickr.com/photos/valuska

★ p6 Katie > flickr.com/photos/babysinblack00 / Julia Priore / Angela Luisa Gutierrez > angelaluisa@gmail.com > flickr: Luisahhh! / Rebecca > no48. blogspot.com

★ p7 C. Cole > greta.grenada@gmail. com > flickr: greta*grenada

★ p8 Francesca Zmetra > thesnailandthecyclops.blogspot.com

★ p9 Natalie Mather > flickr: atriuum

★ p10 Heini Koskinen > flickr.com/photos/piksi_

★ p11 Eden Cayen > flickr.com/photos/ebet

★ p12 Rachael Oglesby > rachael@myheartmyheart.org > flickr: softspoken

★ p13 Bethany Fong > bestfriendenvy. livejournal.com

★ p14 Mary Elam > flickr.com/firefly-path_photography

★ p15 Johanna Öst > johannaost.com

★ p16 Francesca Zmetra > thesnailandthecyclops.blogspot.com

★ p17 Lidia Luna > lidiaon@gmail.com > lunamode.blogspot.com

★ p18 Emily Fontaine > flickr: LaBelleVie

★ p19 Katie > flickr.com/photos/babysinblack00

★ p20 Susanne Hirschmann > flickr: ophelia

★ p21 Stine M. Johnsen > flickr.com/photos/stinemo

★ p22 Stephanie > legs_sadovsky@hotmail.com > flickr.com/photos/guiltyquilty

★ p23 Euvie > university student > 23

★ p24 Kat Bouch > flickr.com/photos/snowkat

★ p25 Jenny Van't Land > flickr: freespiritjenny

★ p26 Ren Rong > flickr: renr > flickr.com/photos/hyakuiro

★ p27 Emily Rose Theobald > Emily. Theobald@yahoo.com > flickr.com/photos/itgirlragdoll

★ p28 Lydia Okello > flickr: lokello

★ p29 Marcine Miller > aclockwithouthands.blogspot.com

★ p30-31 Betty R. Williams

★ p32 Jillian Slater

★ p33 Gala Darling > galadarling.com

★ p34 Ramaida > flickr.com/photos/ramaida

★ p35 Jem Ross > jemibook.blogspot. com > Jemnifur.etsy.com

★ p36 Rebecca Roe Stice > theclothes. blogspot.com

★ p37 Shay Wilson > flickr: Violetwired > photo by Angus Mclellan

★ p38 Stine M. Johnsen > flickr.com/photos/stinemo

★ p39 Christina > closetbug.blogspot. com

★ p40 Amanda Ford > is-mental. blogspot.com > flickr.com/photos/sinceagain

★ p41 Rodellee M > adorevintage.com

★ p42 Elena Duque Viña > flickr. photos/modasanacleta

★ p43 April Leino > flickr: white > whiteapple.etsy.com

★ p44-45 Tetyana K > model and photographer > flickr.com/pho tetyanak

★ p46 Missa > thriftcandy.blogsp com

★ p47 Daphne Jean > flickr: jean quoi

★ p48 Eva Leuenberger > flickr.c photos/ibelieveinunicorns

★ p49 Katherine > flickr: one daaaangerous easter egg

★ p50 Rhainnon Leifheit > liebemarlene.com

★ p51 Rita

★ p52 Lauren Stock > flickr: str match > strike-match.blogspc

★ p53 Lily Greig > lilygreig@gn > flickr.com/photos/lg-photog

★ p54 Heini Koskinen > flickr.c photos/piksi_

★ p55 HannaH Hundley > com/photos/valuska

★ p56 Natalie Mather > flickr:

★ p57 Anne-Solange Tardy > annesolangetardy@gmail.con cachemireetsoie.fr

★ p58 Bethany Fong > bestfrier livejournal.com

★ p59 Nubby Twiglet > nubby nubbytwiglet.com > nubbytv com

★ p60 Madison Hartley > virginia-blue.blogspot.com > ebay:virginiabluevintage

★ p61 Jamie Cassell > flickr.co photos/calmcalmcoma

★ p62 Aarika Hengst > scaarik yahoo.com > flickr.com/pho scaarika

★ p63 Eden Cayen > flickr.c ebet

★ p64 Katarzyna Mirek > nie autograf.pl > flickr: Madika